FRAGMENTE
and
3.31.93.

**Other Chaucer Press Books by Lars Norén
Translated by Marita Lindholm Gochman**

Two Plays: And Give Us the Shadows and *Autumn and Winter*

Three Plays: Demons, Act, and *Terminal 3*

Plays by Lars Norén: Blood and *War*

FRAGMENTE

and

3.31.93.

By

Lars Norén

Translated by

Marita Lindholm Gochman

Chaucer Press Books
An Imprint of Richard Altschuler & Associates, Inc.

Los Angeles

FRAGMENTE and 3.31.93. Copyright © 2017 by Marita Lindholm Gochman. For information and bulk orders write to the publisher, Richard Altschuler & Associates, Inc., at richard.altschuler@gmail.com.

The translation cost for this book was defrayed by a grant from the Swedish Arts Council, gratefully acknowledged.

This English language translation of plays by Lars Norén is published with the permission of the author. All rights reserved. No part of this publication may be reproduced, stored in a retrieval system, or transmitted, in any form or by any means, electronic, mechanical, photocopying, recording, or otherwise, without the prior written permission of Richard Altschuler & Associates, Inc.

ISBN-13: 978-1-884092-95-4

Library of Congress Control Number: 2016963208

CIP data for this book are available from the Library of Congress

Chaucer Press Books is an imprint of Richard Altschuler & Associates, Inc.

Cover Layout and Design: Inspire Creative Works

Printed in the United States of America

Dedication

To our beloved, brilliant grandchildren, Ella, Jeff, Jonas, Nicky, Wini, Mikaela, Beck, Sofia, Karolina, Addy, Henry and Andrew—each one with the capacity to change the world for the better.

Contents

Foreword: Sofia Jupither — viii

Translator's Introduction: Marita Lindholm Gochman — xiii

FRAGMENTE — 1

3.31.93. — 135

Major Plays by Lars Norén — 263

Acknowledgments — 265

Foreword

Sofia Jupither

In May of 2012, I got a phone call that, by now, has shown itself to be somewhat of a turning point in my life. I was asked to take over as director of a monumental theater project at the Folkteatern in Gothenburg, Sweden, a prestige-filled project, which for complicated reasons had lost its original director. There was no time to lose, and I accepted right away. This wasn't anything you could say "no" to—a brand new play by Lars Norén, specifically written for this theater at this particular time. The title of the play was "FRAGMENTE," and it was being coproduced by a number of European theaters. After its world premiere in Gothenburg, the production would travel. Among the cities were Paris, Madrid and Brussels.

A few years earlier, I had the privilege of having been invited by Lars Norén to be Artist in Residence at the Folkteatern in Gothenburg, where he was the Artistic Director. I had directed the world premiere of his play SKALV, and had begun an artistic dialogue with him, which has proven to be very important for me as a director; but little did I know the kind of impact the work on "FRAGMENTE" would have on my life.

As you, dear reader, soon will realize, "FRAGMENTE" is an extraordinary play. As in most of Lars' writing, it has a dialogue that's character-building and character-driven. That part didn't surprise me at all: No one working in the Swedish theater is unaware of the extraordinary gift that Lars has for creating characters by the way they talk (or not talk). No, what knocked me out was the story itself, the little "everyday" hell in closeup, which the text, both cruelly and calmly, but insistently, brings to us. This "everyday" black hole of hopelessness made me flinch. This was "black" in a whole new way: black, but as always in a Norén text, with great tenderness for the characters in the drama, which makes it impossible not to be moved by them.

Neither is it possible to use any of our usual models for rationalizing. There aren't any good or bad people in the play, there isn't any "them" to blame, no solutions that would have worked had they done this or that. There simply isn't anything else but these poor people doing their best within their horrible circumstances, and, like an unstoppable river, event after event follows, leaving them in the darkest corner of hell. And, at the same time, Lars gives us this love for humanity, this tenderness in dealing with human shortcomings, our inability to communicate and our incapability of reaching out to each other the way we long to do. And let's not forget the Norén sense of humor. In the middle of the darkness there's a way with words that makes you smile, or even laugh out loud, from how recognizable it all is.

Truth be told, the short time I had to prepare for the work became a battle not to shut the door to my fragile, little soul, but dare to take on the fate of these poor souls, dare to look at their stories and not just treat them with the cold and professional eye of a stage director. Slowly self-doubt started to creep in. How can I, a middle class, educated woman with a well-behaved son and a little money in the bank, have the right to portray these people? Never before had I even thought about the concept of "representation" on stage—but now "shame" started to burn. Did I even have the right to tell the story of these people?

Halfway into rehearsals it didn't work any longer. I cancelled the Saturday rehearsal, went to Stockholm and asked Lars to meet me for a cup of coffee. By now I doubted everything: Why even theater? Why don't I join Doctors without Borders in Congo? How will I be able to eat breakfast every morning when this kind of horror is happening next to me, in reality, every day? Who am I? Am I a vampire sucking the life stories out of these people just to put a play on stage? How the hell do I have the right to believe that I can do justice to their pain, I, who've never walked in their shoes? What am I made of, thinking that I can direct their hell?

Lars's answer, after this desperate barrage of words, was calm and reassuring. "You have to direct this play just because you know how to do it. I had to write it, just because I knew how to do it. These people can't tell their own stories, but we can, and we are good at it, and therefore it is our responsibility to do it. Otherwise their stories won't be told."

Two days later I returned to Gothenburg and continued the rehearsals with a whole new kind of strength. I suddenly understood why art is important, and that what we do in the theater can make a difference. One week before opening night we invited people from a city shelter to come and watch a tech rehearsal. The actors and I were equally nervous. The feeling of shame and guilt had by now also crept into the ensemble, in spite of my ardent efforts to protect them. But the performance was a success! There were laughs, loud roars and tears in the theater, and among the reactions to the play I especially remember these two: one came from a toothless, worn-out woman, about fifty years old, who laughed and said that she had recognized almost all of her former boyfriends; the other came from a big-eyed, soft-spoken woman, clearly marked by a hard life, who quietly repeated the phrase:"How does he know? Lars Norén, how does he KNOW?"

The production was well received by both critics and audiences in Gothenburg, and was a success in both Paris and Brussels. However, the reception in Madrid, Spain was the one that made the biggest impression on me and the ensemble. We arrived in a Madrid hurting from the aftereffects of the big financial collapse of '08, which had left serious wounds in the Spanish society; and the play, with its tender but naked portrait of people fighting to "hang in," was a home run. Everywhere we met people who said, "You come here from a well-organized Sweden and manage to tell us about us! These are our stories, our pain, our fight!" This is the greatness of Lars, I think, that he, by giving us these close-ups, shows us what it is to be a human being.

A few months later, Lars called and asked if I could read a manuscript that he was currently writing. It was just an early draft, but he wanted me to read it and give him my comments. Of course I felt honored and very happy to oblige. The next day he stood outside my door holding a huge pile of papers with a smile on his face. "Take your time," he said, trying to look like he meant it. It was a given that I would throw myself into the script as soon as we had finished our coffee. "There are ninety-nine scenes that you can do whatever you want with." Those were the words he said when he left, and as evening turned to night, and I had crammed about six hundred (!) pages, I was astonished over how well he knew me. Out from the pages my own home environment popped out— the people who had populated my own life, the anxiety of growing up in the suburbs, a suburb that was divided in the middle by the main road. On one side were the small, identical villas with perfect lawns and shining cars, housing the successful, educated families. On the other side were the low-income apartment houses for those who hadn't really made it. What he had done was to mercilessly focus on this middle layer of society, which never really stands out, never poses any problems and never becomes anything but statistics in the flood of news in the media. He put it into focus and slowly pried open the well-protected surface of ordinariness and, thereby, uncovered the abyss.

I knew right away that I had to direct this play, and a few days later we met again. I told Lars what I thought, that I had a few questions, and that there were a few things I thought could be cut in order to make it clearer. He asked, "Do you want it? It's for you." For once I was speechless. Did I want it? I didn't want anything else!

We agreed the right place for this play would be the Stockholm City Theater, simply because it's the only theater in Sweden with a big, broad ensemble of strong actors, who would appreciate taking part in the kind of extensive project we knew it would be. In "FRAGMENTE," we had used eleven actors, each one playing several roles, but this time I wanted twenty-five actors, one for each character, plus two little children.

Luckily, the head of the Stockholm City Theater understood and appreciated a project like the one we presented to him, and we got what we asked for. As a first step, we wanted to do a reading with all the actors about a year before we were to start rehearsals—and that was given to us. To be able to listen to a text like this one always gives a much better understanding of the material than sitting at a desk reading it.

Now I want to stop and talk about this first reading of the play. It was surrounded by great guardedness and secrecy. No one was to read the material in advance. It had been printed out from Lars' own PDF file, and copies had been made for the exact number of people involved in the reading; they were then carefully counted at every break and at the end of the day, to make sure that no copy got away.

I had spent a long time assigning the roles, trying to understand who was who. The confusion in this first draft of the play was considerable. A man named N in one scene was suddenly named P in another. One named Q was an alcoholic woman, and then, suddenly, Q was a man sitting in a wheelchair. But after a lot of work I had found something I felt was working. Another reason for confusion is the fact that Lars still writes on a typewriter, which means that, for example, if he writes an "a" but it was supposed to be an "o," he just writes the "o" over the "a," and he corrects by writing "xxxxxxx" over the written text, and so on. That means that these early manuscripts are incredibly messy.

So, there we are, twenty-five of Sweden's most well known actors and me, in a very large rehearsal space, sitting around a big table. They are reading lines for the first time, while I am calling out who's going to read what character before each scene—not the best circumstance one would think, but after just three or four lines there are characters emerging; already after a few words the characters are starting to form, and I can see how the actors become their roles in front of my eyes. Like it says in the Bible, "the word became flesh and blood." It's a fantastic experience to see words become flesh and blood in such a concrete and direct way. I also noticed that the actors themselves became engaged and surprised. During the first coffee break, I heard comments like, "It's strange, but the text is happening inside me." "I know this person."

The same thing happened two years later, when I had the pleasure of directing an excerpt of the play in a staged reading in New York. Here is the play in a different language, different actors are sitting in a circle with the same text, and at the first rehearsal I see completely different, but equally truthful, characters immediately take shape. Completely different actors whisper the same surprised comments: "Strange, but the text seems to be happening within me, I know exactly who this person is."

Recently I gave a Master class in Moscow, where I'd chosen scenes from "3.31.93." just to see what would happen. Once again it proved how alike we are: The people I knew from my time growing up in Sweden could just as easily have come from either New Jersey or Moscow.

It turned out that the work on the world premiere of "3.31.93." in Stockholm was harder for me personally than the work on "FRAGMENTE." This time it wasn't about dealing with human suffering outside of myself, but this was to dig deeply into my own life. It was so close to me that it was annoyingly simple to let it in, and I didn't understand until the end of rehearsals why it had affected me the way it did.

The last month of rehearsals happened during the summer. My family had left the city to give me peace and quiet to do my work. I became darker and darker, and I was spinning deeper and deeper into my own pain—but only outside of work. Inside the theater I was experiencing the best time of my life. The power of having twenty-five actors, twenty-five lead actors on stage at the same time, all of them present for the entire four-and-a-half hours, was like conducting a symphony orchestra. The power you feel when you have twenty-five actors keenly listening to, and taking part in, each other's stories, quietly reacting to and following in each other's feelings, is something extraordinary. The power of the theater, when it is at its best, is when all of us, on the stage and inside the theater, live and breathe inside each other's souls for a moment, and for a small window in time, share what it is to be human.

Sofia Jupither
Stockholm July 1, 2016

Translator's Introduction

Marita Lindholm Gochman

Lars Norén's plays "FRAGMENTE" and "3.31.93." were written after the catastrophic, worldwide financial crisis of 2008, which affected Sweden as well as the rest of the world in profound and disastrous ways.

In "FRAGMENTE," Lars gives us a kind of absurd x-ray of what happened to the working class, many of them immigrants, after the financial collapse, and shows us how deeply that particular cross section of society was hit by layoffs and uncertainty. In "3.31.93.," he seems to be investigating a middle class neighborhood in a big city fraught with angst, illness and psychological problems, whose citizens both depend upon and avoid each other. In both plays, horrific, pointless crimes are being committed. I get a feeling that Lars is talking about a "disconnect" between human beings and governmental bureaucracies that are trying desperately, but in vain, to be helpful and caring.

There have been questions about the title of the play "3.31.93." Lars has said that it simply stands for 3 acts, 31 scenes in each act and, therefore, 93 scenes in total. The version of the play printed in this book is based on the world premiere production of "3.31.93." at the Stockholm City Theater. "FRAGMENTE" had its world premiere at Folkteatern in Gothenburg. Both productions had been directed by the talented Swedish director Sofia Jupither. My translation of "FRAGMENTE" is from the play that came out of Lars' IBM typewriter.

The Swedish theater critic Lars Ring recently wrote this about Lars Norén: "Norén is a very Swedish dramatist clearly descended from Strindberg and Bergman—by revealing the personal, thereby making it a universal experience. He is also part of a Scandinavian theater tradition, psychological realism made stronger by updated Freudian ideas. Norén is also creating dream plays, barren and sharp—mercurial moments of transparency."

I remember vividly the day "FRAGMENTE" was sent to me sometime in 2010. I downloaded the play and thought that I would just read a couple of pages. Three hours later I sat by my desk stunned by what I had just experienced. I felt I had read the saddest, darkest play Lars had ever written—and that's after having read Norén plays for over thirty years. I was both deeply moved and horrified. The play seemed to have perfectly captured the mood of the time—a rage against abuse of all kinds, interpersonal as well as societal—cruel with horrific acts of violence. Within a month I had a first draft of a translation.

My dear friend and business partner, Bo Corre, and I gathered together a group of actors (the play consists of more than twenty characters) to do a cold reading of the play. These wonderful, talented actors valiantly took on many different parts and gave me an early understanding of this powerful and complex play. After they finished the reading, their reaction was one of absolute admiration. How was Lars able to capture the desperation of people living without a safety net—and to make all these characters believable? How was it possible to weave in the many problems of being an immigrant in a strange country? However, the feeling among the actors was that this play would never work in America. It was much too brutal, much too dark.

It wasn't until I had finished translating "3.31.93." that I began to think about these two plays as belonging together in one book. Both plays seem to have been born out of a deep need to explore societal systems that don't work. The structure in both plays seems more cinematic than theatrical—Greek tragedy meets contemporary filmmaking. Both plays consist of short scenes, fragments of conversation and interruptions. In "FRAGMENTE," the characters unexpectedly bump up against each other in tight spaces at inopportune times—in stairwells, corridors, taxicabs, hospital rooms, small shabby apartments—while in "3.31.93." the characters seem to have a little more space surrounding them.

The fondness the playwright has for all his characters is palpable, as well as the sense of dark humor with which he looks at these poor souls. These plays give us a clear-eyed, poetic, and sometimes absurd view of our human condition. A Swedish theater critic described "3.31.93." as "an angst ridden close up of our world today." I think that statement rings true for both plays.

Translating Norén's language (a language which, by the way, has become a Swedish concept of its own, i.e., one speaks "Norén" in Sweden at certain moments) is to try to understand the characters by taking into account their age, socioeconomic status, and the particular situation they are in. Many times the words themselves have to be tossed out, while you search for expressions that these particular characters would use. Norén's Swedish language is a heightened "everyday" Swedish He has a perfect ear for how contemporary Swedes "talk." My effort is to try to find an equivalent way of expressing how Americans "talk." I have also tried to keep the sparseness, simplicity and economy of words that Lars has used in writing these two plays.

I recently read something that Robert Alter, the English translator of the great Israeli poet Yehuda Amichai, wrote about translations, which rang true to me. "The work is arduous, necessary and unfinished, references, puns, jokes, buried meanings—the creases of a culture, its age lines are inevitably smoothed out of existence in translation."

What really stands out about "FRAGMENTE" and "3.31.93." is their humanity—how both plays capture our everyday lives, for better or worse. As my friend Bo said after having seen "3.31.93.": "I went down in the subway and I felt as if the play was still going on around me." Lars seems to feel that we haven't come very far as civilized human beings, but there is also a sense of forgiveness—a tiny ray of hope shining through the plays, mostly from his young, female characters.

Someone in Sweden wrote that many playwrights hold up a mirror to society but Lars Norén holds up a mirror to the human soul.

A few more thoughts about the plays: Lars expressed, in an anthology of his plays published in Sweden, which included "FRAGMENTE" and "3.31.93.," that he was trying to create a tapestry of human lives. He wrote these two plays after 2008, as mentioned, but before the Syrian crisis. By holding up a mirror to a troubled society, where answers to our problems seem almost impossible to find, Lars has given us, as in a Greek drama, the possibility of a catharsis. The American stage director David Esbjornson, after having read "3.31.93.," said that "the play is an homage to humanity."

To me, both plays are contemporary Greek tragedies: plays of catastrophes, on both a small and large scale, about human beings who are constantly beaten down—by their own actions, by a cruel welfare system, or by being part of harmful family patterns. The plays are clear-eyed, poetic, and sometimes absurd x-rays of our human condition.

What seems abstract and confusing on the page becomes surprisingly clear once realized on stage. Lars has said that it is important to make the audience aware that there is no story being told on stage—to deprive the audience of their expectations of dramatic content and events leading up to an explanation.

FRAGMENTE

Characters

THE GIRL
THE BOY
THE MAN
THE MOM
THE YOUNG ONE
THE MOTHER
HENRY
THE DAUGHTER
THE PREGNANT NURSE
THE DOCTOR
THE NEIGHBOR
THE WIFE OF THE NEIGHBOR
THE OTHER
THE OLD ONE
THE MOTHER OF THE GIRL
THE PASTOR
THE OTHER MOTHER
THE WIFE OF THE PASTOR
THE OLD WOMAN
BENNY
THE YOUNG WOMAN
THE FRIEND
THE OTHER ONE
THE OLDER FATHER
THE YOUNG DAUGHTER
THE OLDER MOTHER
THE OLDEST SON
THE SISTER
THE ELDER
THE FRIEND OF THE MOTHER OF THE GIRL
THE IRANIAN
THE OLD IRANIAN
THE LITTLE ONE
THE BROTHER
SELUAH
YASMIN
THE SWEDE
THE LITTLE BOY
THE HALF-DRESSED MAN
THE PREGNANT ONE
THE MOTHER OF THE PREGNANT ONE
MIDDLE-AGED MAN
THE FIRST GUARD
THE SECOND GUARD

A BIG, BLACK ROOM.
MERCILESS LIGHT.

("THE GIRL" IS WALKING ALONG THE STAGE, NOTICES "THE BOY," WAITS FOR HIM. THE BOY, ALSO WALKING, NOTICES HER, STOPS, STARTS TO WALK IN ANOTHER DIRECTION.)

THE GIRL: Stop.

THE BOY: What?

THE GIRL: Why the hell don't you stop when I say so?

THE BOY: Why?

THE GIRL: It's you, isn't it? It's you.

THE BOY: What?

THE GIRL: Who called. It's you, right?

THE BOY: Called?

THE GIRL: Where did you get my cellphone number?

THE BOY: I didn't.

THE GIRL: Who the hell gave it to you? My number is unlisted. Who gave it to you?

THE BOY: I don't know your number.

THE GIRL: I said who the hell gave it to you?

THE BOY: I don't have it. I don't know your number.

THE GIRL: I've checked. It's you.

THE BOY: No.

THE GIRL: I know it's you.

THE BOY: No, it's not me.

THE GIRL: I called you at home. I've got your number. Your Mom answered.

THE BOY: It's not me.

THE GIRL: It sure is. You've called me many, many times. You called me at 12:30 last night. You did. It's disgusting.

THE BOY: No.

THE GIRL: And sent pictures.

THE BOY: No. Cut it out.

THE GIRL: To me.

THE BOY: Why would I?

THE GIRL: Because you're like that.

THE BOY: No.

THE GIRL: It's disgusting. You're disgusting.

(SILENCE)

THE GIRL: I'll show them to my dad.

THE BOY: So, why don't you?

THE GIRL: I know that it was you who called and sent the pictures.

THE BOY: Really.

THE GIRL: Now I've got to get a new number and everything—so that you'll leave me alone.

THE BOY: Why don't you do that.

THE GIRL: I'll show them to everyone in school. You're a pervert.

THE BOY: I haven't done anything. I'm innocent.

THE GIRL: You aren't innocent. You're disgusting.

(THE BOY BENDS DOWN, PICKS UP A BIG ROCK AND HITS HER ON HER HEAD. HE CONTINUES TO HIT HER UNTIL SHE IS DEAD, ENDS UP SITTING ON TOP OF HER, THEN STANDS UP WHEN IT'S OVER AND WALKS AWAY.)

■

(THE BOY IS STANDING OUTSIDE THE ROOM LISTENING.)

THE MAN: (SITTING IN A CHAIR ACROSS FROM THE MOM.) You don't have a lot of furniture, do you?

THE MOM: No.

THE MAN: Almost nothing left. Right?

THE MOM: Yea, they came and picked them up when I couldn't pay.

THE MAN: You couldn't pay?

THE MOM: No, I didn't . . . I didn't have enough . . .

THE MAN: No, it's rough.

THE MOM: Rainer needs new clothes.

THE MAN: Where is the dog?

THE MOM: The dog?

THE MAN: Yes.

THE MOM: What dog?

THE MAN: That white one he had. A little, white fucking dog that was always yelping and dropping blood.

THE MOM: Tessa?

THE MAN: Tessa?

THE MOM: You know. I know you know. (LISTENS) There's someone there.

THE MAN: What? Know what? It was so long ago. Everything. (PUTS HIS LEFT HAND BETWEEN THE LEGS OF THE MOM.)

(SILENCE)

THE MOM: No.

THE MAN: Yes. (SILENCE) Yes . . . what's wrong? Rainer? What's wrong?

(SILENCE)

THE MOM: Are you there?

THE MAN: Is he here?

THE MOM: Why don't you answer me?

(SILENCE)

THE MOM: Rainer?

THE BOY: What?

THE MOM: Come here.

THE BOY: Why? (SHORT PAUSE) What do you want? (COMES IN TO THE ROOM.)

THE MAN: Hi, there. (SILENCE)

THE MOM: It's Arvid.

THE MAN: That's me. How are you?

THE MOM: He brought me flowers. White tulips.

THE MAN: You used to like them.

THE MOM: Yes . . .ten of them.

THE MAN: You used to anyway.

THE MOM: These days one can't afford them anymore . . . the way it is.

THE MAN: So, how are you, Rainer? (SILENCE) Rainer?

THE MOM: That was my dad's name. Answer him.

THE MAN: (STOPS MASSAGING THE MOM'S CROTCH.) He never says a fucking thing.

THE MOM: No, he's mostly silent.

THE MAN: He's getting bigger.

THE MOM: Yes, he's almost fifteen.

THE MAN: He is?

THE MOM: Yes, in December.

THE MAN: Yes, time flies. Come here. Come and sit here.

THE MOM: I have to buy him new shoes. He's walking around in his old sneakers he's had for years . . . . Yes, the ones he's wearing. But I haven't had the money. Now there's snow . . .

THE MAN: Well, that's the way it is.

(SILENCE)

THE MOM: You try the best you can, but that's not always enough.

THE MAN: No, you do what you can.

THE MOM: More than that you can't do.

THE MAN: What else is new?

THE MOM: We got a little money from the Salvation Army. Otherwise we'd have gone under.

THE MAN: Good for you, you have your faith anyway.

THE MOM: Yes, but . . .

THE MAN: That's the only thing you have.

THE MOM: Yes, but . . .

THE MAN: You know, you should get yourself some new teeth. (SILENCE) I guess it's not easy to find a new job the way things are.

THE MOM: No, it isn't.

THE MAN: Things don't look very bright.

THE MOM: I'd worked there for twelve years. Four of us were laid off the same day. No explanation. Didn't even get the vacation money they owed us. Don't know what's going to happen. You don't know what to do.

THE BOY: Where's Sanna?

THE MOM: What am I to do?

THE MAN: Well, I don't know.

THE BOY: Where's Sanna?

THE MOM: Sanna? She isn't here.

THE MAN: Where is she?

THE MOM: I guess she'll be here soon. They'll let her out for the weekend.

THE BOY: If you touch her I'll kill you.

■

THE MAN: How's it going? (SILENCE) Don't you feel well? (PAUSE) Are you sick or something?

THE YOUNG ONE: Who?

THE MAN: You. Are you drunk? You can't sit here. (HE TOUCHES HER.) Do you need help? (SHORT PAUSE) Do you hear me? (TOUCHES HER.) How're you doing?

THE YOUNG ONE: Oh shit, I'm dying.

THE MAN: You are?

THE YOUNG ONE: Yes.

THE MAN: No, don't die.

THE YOUNG ONE: Where are my . . .

THE MAN: Did you piss yourself?

THE YOUNG ONE: Where are my children?

THE MAN: Do you live here?

THE YOUNG ONE: Stella and . . .

THE MAN: Who?

THE YOUNG ONE: Stella?

THE MAN: Stella? Who's Stella?

THE YOUNG ONE: Stella and . . . Liam.

THE MAN: (TOUCHES HER AGAIN. TRIES TO LIFT HER FACE UP.) Don't you want to come home with me instead? Much more fun.

THE YOUNG ONE: (VAGUELY SHAKES HER HEAD.) No.

THE MAN: Come with me. Come. (SILENCE) What do you say?

THE YOUNG ONE: Where are they?

THE MAN: Come home . . . with me.

(PAUSE)

THE MAN: Let me see . . . let me see what you look like?

THE YOUNG ONE: Yes. (SLOWLY STANDS UP, WALKS UP TO ONE OF THE DOORS, STARTS TO KNOCK ON THE DOOR.)

THE MAN: Let's see if you're worth shit. . . . Are you?

THE YOUNG ONE: Open . . . open the door.

THE MAN: Do you live here?

THE YOUNG ONE: Please open the door.

THE MAN: No one wants to open for you. Fucking whore. (LEAVES)

∎

THE YOUNG ONE: Can I come in?

THE MOTHER: Is that you?

THE YOUNG ONE: Can I?

THE MOTHER: It's been so long.

THE YOUNG ONE: Yes.

(SILENCE)

THE YOUNG ONE: I'm sorry.

THE MOTHER: Sure. That's easy to say.

(SILENCE)

THE MOTHER: Was that you knocking?

THE YOUNG ONE: On the door?

THE MOTHER: Yes . . . a while ago. I was resting. I was working the night shift. I thought I heard someone knocking.

THE YOUNG ONE: Yes.

(SILENCE)

THE MOTHER: So, what now?

THE YOUNG ONE: I don't know.

THE MOTHER: Aha.

(SILENCE)

THE YOUNG ONE: Well . . . Mike.

THE MOTHER: Aha.

THE YOUNG ONE: That's what has happened.

THE MOTHER: Oh God, what now?

THE YOUNG ONE: He threw me out. Last night. Again. I've been walking around all night. I had no place to go.

THE MOTHER: Look, I'm on my way out. That's why I'm wearing a coat.

THE YOUNG ONE: I don't know where to go. I was walking around all night—thinking of Stella and Liam. That's all I was thinking about.

THE MOTHER: I have to be at work at ten. Then I have to work tonight again. We don't have enough people as it is.

THE YOUNG ONE: I don't know what to do.

THE MOTHER: No . . . I don't either.

THE YOUNG ONE: He hit me . . . he never did that before. Hit me, I mean.

THE MOTHER: Why?

THE YOUNG ONE: I don't know. He was fired because he's been coming in late too often. And then he borrowed money all over the place to buy a car so that he could get a new job.

THE MOTHER: Why did he do that? He has a car.

THE YOUNG ONE: They took it because he wasn't able to keep up the payments.

THE MOTHER: On the one he has?

THE YOUNG ONE: Yes, on the one he had. The one he doesn't have anymore.

THE MOTHER: I see.

THE YOUNG ONE: Is it OK if I stay here for a while? I'll just sit here. I won't do anything. Just sit here. And get warmed up. For a little while.

THE MOTHER: Yes, but I'm leaving.

THE YOUNG ONE: I thought I'd freeze to death. I've no shoes. I was standing on the bridge . . . but then I thought I'd go to the emergency room, but I couldn't find my way and then I just walked around and I must've fallen asleep somewhere. It felt like my tears were frozen to my cheeks.

THE MOTHER: I'm working all night.

THE YOUNG ONE: I'm just going to sit here. I don't want to do anything—just sit here and get warm.

THE MOTHER: Then tomorrow, when I'm done, I'm going over to Mia. We're driving out to do a big shopping at the Food Co-op.

THE YOUNG ONE: If it hadn't been for Stella and Liam I'd have jumped. Right down on the railway tracks. They were the first thing I thought of this morning, and that's why I went home. Otherwise I wouldn't have gone home. But he wouldn't open the door.

THE MOTHER: Sure, you can stay here for a couple of hours.

THE YOUNG ONE: I don't know where they are. (SILENCE) No one answered the door.

■

THE MOTHER: Are you sitting here?

HENRY: Yes, I am.

THE MOTHER: Why aren't you sleeping?

HENRY: No, I'm not sleeping.

THE MOTHER: Why not?

HENRY: Why not?

THE MOTHER: Well, I'm going to sleep anyway.

HENRY: That's fine. Why don't you get some sleep?

THE MOTHER: I worked all night long.

HENRY: Me too. . . . What do think I've been doing? (SILENCE) What do you think I've been doing?

THE MOTHER: Why were you just sitting downstairs?

HENRY: Where?

THE MOTHER: In the car . . . in the parking lot. Why were you sitting down there for such a long time, in the car?

HENRY: Long time?

THE MOTHER: What were you doing?

HENRY: What I was doing? I was counting up the tips.
THE MOTHER: You just sat there. You didn't do anything. You just sat there.

HENRY: I was counting my money. What do you think I was doing?

THE MOTHER: I don't know. That's why I'm asking.

HENRY: I was counting my money. I was counting how little I'd made. A hell of a lot less than I should've made. Just seventy-five bucks. Seventy-five bucks for a whole fucking night. From eleven to seven in the morning.

(SILENCE)

THE MOTHER: I saw that you were doing something.

HENRY: What the fuck do you mean?

THE MOTHER: I don't know . . .

HENRY: What the fuck could I be doing in the front seat of a taxi?

THE MOTHER: Your hands were in the dark.

HENRY: In the dark?

THE MOTHER: One couldn't see them.

HENRY: So, you didn't see them.

THE MOTHER: I saw your face.

HENRY: Oh hell, just stop it.

THE MOTHER: But I saw your face.

HENRY: Yea, about time. (SILENCE) What do you want?

THE MOTHER: Nothing.

HENRY: What was I doing?

THE MOTHER: I don't know.

HENRY: No, you don't know. There's a lot you don't know.

THE MOTHER: Your hands were in the dark.

HENRY: In the dark?

THE MOTHER: So one couldn't see them.

HENRY: So you didn't see them then.

THE MOTHER: I saw your face.

HENRY: You don't know anything.

THE MOTHER: I saw your face.

HENRY: My face?

THE MOTHER: Yes . . . I saw it.

(SILENCE)

HENRY: So what?

THE MOTHER: I didn't recognize it.

HENRY: No.

THE MOTHER: It wasn't you.

HENRY: No. (SILENCE) Who was it then?

THE MOTHER: Were you sitting there jerking off?

HENRY: Jerking off?

THE MOTHER: Yes, is that what you were doing . . . at your age?

HENRY: No, unfortunately not.
THE MOTHER: Were you sitting by yourself in the car jerking off instead of coming up to my bed—for hours?

HENRY: Sounds too good to be true.

THE MOTHER: I saw it . . . I saw your hands. How they moved.

HENRY: These? (SHOWS HER HIS HANDS, WHICH ARE BLOODY AND WOUNDED.)

(SILENCE)

HENRY: I've been driving the whole fucking night since nine o'clock last night in this fucking snowstorm, or I've been sitting outside some fucking bar waiting for some drunken, spoiled sucker to be taken home to some fucking fancy apartment building, and he treats you like you were dog shit; and then around five in the morning I got a ride from one of those fucking parasites who started to complain that he smelled smoke in the car, and that the meter was wrong, and that the ride was taking too long; and then he tried to run away without paying; and then I got out of the car and pulled him out of the backseat and hit him to a pulp with my own two hands. I hit him until he was on his knees and I didn't have any more strength left to go on, and then I drove home. Then I sat in the car and thought about what I'd become, and what good it does to try to do the right thing. I don't know if he's dead or alive and I don't give a shit either way. It's all the same to me. I don't regret anything.

■

HENRY: It's me. (SILENCE) How's it going? (SILENCE) Agnes? (PAUSE) How are things?

THE DAUGHTER: What do you want, old cunt?

HENRY: What I want?

THE DAUGHTER: What do you want?

HENRY: I want to see you.

THE DAUGHTER: Why?

HENRY: Because . . . Well, you know.

THE DAUGHTER: Why?

HENRY: I want to see how you are?

THE DAUGHTER: How am I?

HENRY: Yes . . . How are things? (SHORT PAUSE) How do you feel?

THE DAUGHTER: Fine.

HENRY: Fine?

THE DAUGHTER: Yes.

HENRY: Aha.

THE DAUGHTER: How are you doing?

HENRY: Well . . .

THE DAUGHTER: Cunt.

HENRY: Aha. (SILENCE) What do the doctors say?

THE DAUGHTER: What doctors?

HENRY: The ones that work here . . . the ones you see.

THE DAUGHTER: There aren't any here, cunt.

HENRY: Don't they tell you anything?

THE DAUGHTER: Who?

HENRY: The doctors, the physicians.

THE DAUGHTER: No. They don't say anything.

HENRY: No?

THE DAUGHTER: No, they don't say anything. They haven't said anything. Have they?

HENRY: No, not to me.

THE DAUGHTER: What do you want?

HENRY: What do I want?

THE DAUGHTER: What do you want?

HENRY: I want to see you.

THE DAUGHTER: Well, now you've seen me.

HENRY: Yes.

THE DAUGHTER: You can leave now.

HENRY: Yes, yes. Soon

THE DAUGHTER: When are you leaving?

HENRY: Soon. Not now. I just got here. I want to talk to you.

THE DAUGHTER: Why? (SILENCE) Why?

HENRY: Well . . .

THE DAUGHTER: Why?

HENRY: Everything is fine.

THE DAUGHTER: It's cunt.

HENRY: Sure . . .

THE DAUGHTER: Do you want to see cunt?

HENRY: No.

THE DAUGHTER: So why are you here?

HENRY: Quiet. Don't talk like that.

THE DAUGHTER: What do you want to see then? That's all I got!

HENRY: Nothing. I just want to talk to you for a little while. Just sit and talk with you, since I am your father. I am your dad. There's only you and me. There's only you and me left.

THE DAUGHTER: This? (SHOWS HER NAKED WRISTS.) Look. Do you see?

HENRY: Yes, I see.

THE DAUGHTER: You do?

HENRY: Yes.

THE DAUGHTER: That's for real. But you're used to it. I guess it's nothing to you. That it means nothing.

HENRY: It must've hurt like hell.

THE DAUGHTER: No, it felt good. Fucking good.

HENRY: Good?

THE DAUGHTER: Very good.

HENRY: Aha.

THE DAUGHTER: Are you leaving now?

HENRY: No. No, I'm not leaving. . . . Do you want to go for a smoke?

THE DAUGHTER: No.

HENRY: Maybe in a little while. (SILENCE) Do you remember when you were a little girl? . . . You used to say . . .

THE DAUGHTER: I was never a little girl.

HENRY: When you were a little girl . . . when I came home . . . the thing you really loved, you and Slobodan . . . was when your dad took a bath with the two of you . . . that gave you the greatest joy . . .

THE DAUGHTER: That's when you touched my cunt.

HENRY: I haven't touched anything.

THE DAUGHTER: Fucking murderer.

HENRY: I'm not.

THE DAUGHTER: Fucking murderer. How many have you killed?

HENRY: I haven't murdered anyone. Not a single one.

THE DAUGHTER: One hundred, two hundred, even more?

HENRY: There was a war. You don't understand.

THE DAUGHTER: Fucking murderer.

HENRY: I just wanted to save all of you, your mother, you, Slobodan, Grandma and Grandpa. . . . What else could I have done? (LONG SILENCE) Now you and I are the only ones left. (SHORT PAUSE) And a few old buddies at the café. That's all I have. (SILENCE) I need a cigarette. Are you coming or not?

THE DAUGHTER: I have no cigarettes.

HENRY: I do.

THE DAUGHTER: I have no money . . . no work. Nowhere to live. Nothing. That's what I have. Nothing.

HENRY: Let's go for a smoke.

THE DAUGHTER: OK.

HENRY: Come on.

THE DAUGHTER: To forget?

HENRY: There's nothing to forget.

(THEY GO OUT TO THE CORRIDOR, WHERE THEY BUMP INTO THE PREGNANT NURSE AND THE DOCTOR.)

THE DAUGHTER: We're going for a smoke.

THE PREGNANT NURSE: Yes, why not.

THE DAUGHTER: That's all I do here. That's my only therapy. The only therapy I get here.

THE PREGNANT NURSE: Is that right?

THE DAUGHTER: You bet that's right.

THE DOCTOR: Are you leaving?

THE PREGNANT NURSE: Seems that way. I'm going home.

THE DOCTOR: Well . . .sleep good.

THE PREGNANT NURSE: And you're just starting?

THE DOCTOR: Yes, seems so.

THE PREGNANT NURSE: Did you plan it that way?

THE DOCTOR: Sorry?

THE DAUGHTER: This is my dad.

THE PREGNANT NURSE: I know. We've met before. A couple of times.

HENRY: I've been here almost every day.

THE DAUGHTER: He's a taxi driver.

THE PREGNANT NURSE: Aha.

THE DAUGHTER: And a murderer. From Belgrade.

THE PREGNANT NURSE: That's a good job.

THE DAUGHTER: Murderer?

THE PREGNANT NURSE: Taxi driver.

THE DOCTOR: You meet a lot of people.

THE DAUGHTER: Like here.

HENRY: Yes, you have to be a little like a therapist, too.

THE DAUGHTER: Why don't you get a job here then?

HENRY: Yes, maybe I could.

THE DAUGHTER: Doesn't take a lot. Mostly that you're on time.

HENRY: Come on. Let's go.

(THEY WALK AWAY.)

THE DOCTOR: She's full of pep, anyway.

THE PREGNANT NURSE: She is?

THE DOCTOR: Better.

THE PREGNANT NURSE: Better is good.

THE DOCTOR: I can just imagine what he's experienced. . . . He looks like he came directly out of a war documentary.

THE PREGNANT NURSE: Did you plan this?

THE DOCTOR: Plan it? What?

THE PREGNANT NURSE: That you start when I leave?

THE DOCTOR: I'm not in charge of scheduling.

THE PREGNANT NURSE: Almost looks like it. So, when you said you love me . . .

THE DOCTOR: What did I say?

THE PREGNANT NURSE: Yesterday. In your apartment. That you love me. You said you love me.

THE DOCTOR: What did I mean by that?

THE PREGNANT NURSE: When you said it, you said, "and only you." You said you love me and only me.

THE DOCTOR: I did?

THE PREGNANT NURSE: So what did you mean?

THE DOCTOR: I don't know, really.

THE PREGNANT NURSE: When you say, "Only me," is that because you want to tell me there's someone else too, but that I'm the only one you love, and that you're finally realizing that?

THE DOCTOR: Realizing that?

THE PREGNANT NURSE: Is that what you mean? (SHORT PAUSE) Why did you say, "Only me?"

THE DOCTOR: Can't we talk about this later?

THE PREGNANT NURSE: Why? I'm leaving.

THE DOCTOR: That's what I mean. You're going home to your husband.

THE PREGNANT NURSE: Where else could I go? I've nowhere else to go. (SHORT PAUSE) But he's not home. He's not back until Thursday

THE DOCTOR: When are you going to talk to him?

THE PREGNANT NURSE: On Thursday. When he's home.

THE DOCTOR: You've got to.

THE PREGNANT NURSE: Yes, I know. (STANDS UP. WE SEE THAT SHE IS PREGNANT.) I'm so tired.

THE DOCTOR: I noticed.

THE PREGNANT NURSE: She's awake now. (PUTS HER HAND ON HER STOMACH.) Did you see that?

THE DOCTOR: No. (THE PREGNANT NURSE TAKES HIS HAND AND PUTS IT ON HER STOMACH.) Yes, I feel something. . . . What is it?

THE PREGNANT NURSE: What does it feel like?

THE DOCTOR: A foot.

THE PREGNANT NURSE: Yes. (SILENCE) She holds her arms just like you . . . the way you do. (SHORT PAUSE) Will I see you tonight?

THE DOCTOR: I hope so. (LOOKS AROUND.) I'm so tired of people who don't make anything of their lives.

THE PREGNANT NURSE: Is that why you work here?

THE DOCTOR: I guess so.

■

(THE PREGNANT NURSE MEETS HER NEIGHBOR.)

THE NEIGHBOR: (PUTS DOWN A COUPLE OF BIG SHOPPING BAGS.) How's it going?

THE PREGNANT NURSE: Slowly.

THE NEIGHBOR: I guess congratulations are in place.

THE PREGNANT NURSE: Thank you.

THE NEIGHBOR: So, when are you due?

THE PREGNANT NURSE: In two months, I hope.

THE NEIGHBOR: Yes, yes. (SHORT PAUSE) I was just thinking . . . if you haven't already gotten a crib, we have an old one in the basement that's been there for a while—but maybe you already have one. I guess this is your first?

THE PREGNANT NURSE: A crib?

THE NEIGHBOR: Perfectly fine.

THE PREGNANT NURSE: Yes, I . . .

THE NEIGHBOR: Don't think we'll have any more use for . . . the way things are . . . I mean.

THE PREGNANT NURSE: Maybe that would be good . . . later I mean.

THE NEIGHBOR: Why don't you go down and take a look at it?

THE PREGNANT NURSE: Thank you. Very kind of you.

THE NEIGHBOR: I guess I have a reason for it. It would be good to get rid of it. That would give us some more room down there. There's hardly room for the winter tires. I'm just bringing this upstairs. Then I'll get Lena.

THE PREGNANT NURSE: Is she at home?

THE NEIGHBOR: No. She's sitting in the car.

THE PREGNANT NURSE: How's she?

THE NEIGHBOR: She wanted to come home. At this point she wanted to come home. To be at home.

THE PREGNANT NURSE: She did?

THE NEIGHBOR'S WIFE: (COMES UP THE STAIRS.) I wanted to come home.

THE NEIGHBOR: Much better to be home.

THE PREGNANT NURSE: Are you sure you want to be home?
THE NEIGHBOR'S WIFE: I'm sure.

THE PREGNANT NURSE: Yes, sorry, I . . .

THE NEIGHBOR'S WIFE: But it's hard to understand.

THE NEIGHBOR: I understand.

THE NEIGHBOR'S WIFE: Are you pregnant?

THE NEIGHBOR: You knew that. I told you. Many times. I told you she was pregnant.

THE NEIGHBOR'S WIFE: How nice.

THE PREGNANT NURSE: Yes.

THE NEIGHBOR'S WIFE: Life continues. . . . There's one more bag downstairs.

THE NEIGHBOR: Yes, I'll get it. You were supposed to wait in the car.

THE NEIGHBOR'S WIFE: You were taking so long.

THE NEIGHBOR: Yes, but you shouldn't . . .

THE NEIGHBOR'S WIFE: But we're in no hurry.

THE NEIGHBOR: Wait. (WANTS TO HELP HER WALK UPSTAIRS.)

THE NEIGHBOR'S WIFE: No, I'll do it myself. I want to walk by myself as long as I can.

THE NEIGHBOR: Sure, sure.

THE NEIGHBOR'S WIFE: You know it's a wig, don't you?

THE PREGNANT NURSE: What?

THE NEIGHBOR'S WIFE: This one. This terrible thing. You know it's a wig, don't you.

THE PREGNANT NURSE: It is?

THE NEIGHBOR'S WIFE: You know it is.

THE PREGNANT NURSE: No, I didn't think about it.

THE NEIGHBOR'S WIFE: Well, it is.

THE PREGNANT NURSE: Yes, it is.

THE NEIGHBOR'S WIFE: You do remember what I looked like, don't you?

THE PREGNANT NURSE: Yes, I . . .

THE NEIGHBOR'S WIFE: I miss my hair.

THE NEIGHBOR: It might grow back. You never know.

THE NEIGHBOR'S WIFE: It's pathetic, but I miss it terribly.

THE NEIGHBOR: Yes, but now we have to . . .

THE PREGNANT NURSE: Yes . . . See you soon, see you.

THE NEIGHBOR'S WIFE: Of course we will.

THE NEIGHBOR: Yes, of course. (SILENCE) Good luck.

■

THE NEIGHBOR: Do you have a cigarette?

THE OTHER: Here you are.

THE NEIGHBOR: Thank you.

THE OTHER: They are yours.

THE NEIGHBOR: They are?

THE OTHER: You put them there. You forgot them.

THE NEIGHBOR: I did?

THE OTHER: Last time . . . Since you can't smoke at home. (SILENCE) How are things?

THE NEIGHBOR: I don't know. (SILENCE)

THE OTHER: You don't know?

THE NEIGHBOR: (SHAKES HIS HEAD.)

THE OTHER: So you want to end this?

THE NEIGHBOR: End this?

THE OTHER: Yes, end us.

THE NEIGHBOR: I do?

THE OTHER: What do you want to do?

THE NEIGHBOR: What I want . . .

THE OTHER: Yes, what do you want?

THE NEIGHBOR: Want?

THE OTHER: What about you and me?

THE NEIGHBOR: I don't know. I don't know what I want. This is all I have.

THE OTHER: It's so silly. . . . What is really ending? A couple of fucks now and then for lack of anything else.

THE NEIGHBOR: It's just . . . right now I can't . . . the way things . . .

THE OTHER: No.

THE NEIGHBOR: You understand, don't you?

THE OTHER: Sure I do. I haven't said anything. (SILENCE)

THE NEIGHBOR: She's at home now. I brought her home yesterday. She's in the apartment. She's just there! Hardly anything left, of anything. I mean, not only of her. I don't know what to say to her. What's there to talk about? It's as if she knew.

THE OTHER: About us? Us two?

THE NEIGHBOR: About everything. But we don't say anything.

THE OTHER: Of course she knows. You just know those things.

THE NEIGHBOR: No, she doesn't know what she knows.

THE OTHER: Even before it happens . . . you know. (SILENCE) Ivan is home too. He came home last night.

THE NEIGHBOR: Really.

THE OTHER: Last night. He didn't say a word. Not this morning either. I asked how it had been . . . where he had been . . . but he didn't answer. Just looked at me. I had to say something. (SILENCE) He knows as well.

THE NEIGHBOR: Did you say something?

THE OTHER: No . . . what's there to say? (SILENCE) I'll just leave, if you want me to. I don't know why I haven't done it already.

THE NEIGHBOR: No.

THE OTHER: It won't work. He'll never let me go. He told me that. He says he'd rather kill me.

THE NEIGHBOR: Those are things you say.

THE OTHER: It is? (SHORT PAUSE) Did you ever say that to someone, that you'd rather kill her than let her go?

THE NEIGHBOR: I never had to.

THE OTHER: Maybe it'll still happen. (SILENCE)

THE NEIGHBOR: I'll just continue lying . . . until it's over. At least I don't have to lie to you.

THE OTHER: No, I guess I just have to be strong and deal with it all.

THE NEIGHBOR: She doesn't want to take any medicine any more. No morphine. Nothing. She wants to be clear headed.

(SILENCE)

THE OTHER: We can't stand here any longer.

THE NEIGHBOR: She wants to let go, she says.

THE OTHER: My break is over. I have to go. Bye. ("THE NEIGHBOR" GREETS THE PREGNANT DOCTOR WE MET EARLIER WHO PASSES BY.) What? Do you know her?

THE NEIGHBOR: Yes, she's a neighbor. She lives above us in the same house.

THE OTHER: She's in the ER, I think.

■

("THE OTHER" RUNS INTO "THE MAN" FROM AN EARLIER SCENE, WHO GOES INTO A DARKISH ROOM WHERE AN OLD MAN IS LYING ON HIS BACK STARING UP AT THE CEILING, HIS ARMS ACROSS HIS CHEST AS IF HE WERE DEAD. "THE MAN" SITS QUIETLY DOWN ON A CHAIR NEXT TO THE BED.)

THE OLD ONE: (AS IF HE CAME BACK TO REALITY AND CLARITY AFTER WAKING UP. TURNS HIS HEAD TOWARD THE MAN, LOOKS AT HIM.) Yes?

(SILENCE)

THE OLD ONE: (LIFTS ONE HAND) What is it?

THE MAN: It's me.

THE OLD ONE: Cleaning again?

THE MAN: Cleaning?

THE OLD ONE: You cleaned yesterday.

THE MAN: It's me.

THE OLD ONE: You?

THE MAN: Yes . . . don't you see? It's me.

THE OLD ONE: Really, who are you?

THE MAN: Arvid.

THE OLD ONE: Arvid?

THE MAN: Yes.

THE OLD ONE: Are you here?

THE MAN: Yes, Hedvig told me you were here and that you have skeletal cancer or prostate cancer. Hedvig was the one who told me.

THE OLD ONE: She did? Hedvig?

THE MAN: Yes, the one I was going with . . . who works at the Co-op.

THE OLD ONE: Really.

THE MAN: But she was just fired. Let go.

(SILENCE)

THE OLD ONE: Are you here?

THE MAN: Yes, it seems that way.

THE OLD ONE: I thought I was dreaming.

THE MAN: No. (SILENCE) I had nothing to do . . . thought I might come and see you . . . that's the least one could do . . . since you don't have that much time left.

THE OLD ONE: No.

(SILENCE)

THE MAN: So how are you?

(SILENCE)

THE OLD ONE: How I am? How I am?

(SILENCE)

THE MAN: I guess it was a while since we saw each other.

THE OLD ONE: Yes, it was . . .

THE MAN: Whenever it was.

THE OLD ONE: I didn't know . . .

THE MAN: No.

(SILENCE)

THE MAN: How long have you been here?

THE OLD ONE: Where?

THE MAN: Here.

THE OLD ONE: Oh here . . .

THE MAN: Yes.

THE OLD ONE: I've been waiting for you.

THE MAN: For me?

THE OLD ONE: Yes.

THE MAN: Aha. Really. Why?

THE OLD ONE: All these years.

THE MAN: Aha.

THE OLD ONE: I thought I'd never see you again.

THE MAN: Me neither.

THE OLD ONE: I didn't think I'd ever see you again . . . once more.

THE MAN: No, it . . . (SILENCE, THE OLD ONE CLOSES HIS EYES.) Are you sleeping? (SILENCE) Now I have a good job. Very busy. I'm driving containers down south . . . Good money. Enough. The rich ones want their stuff. So I drive. Night and day. Used to it. And I moved back in with Betty. I guess one has to give it a try. Since we have kids. But the boy isn't happy about it.

THE OLD ONE: What did you say?

THE MAN: The boy isn't very happy that I'm back. He'd rather be the man of the house . . . and do whatever he wants.

THE OLD ONE: What did you say?

THE MAN: Didn't you hear me? (SILENCE) What did you say?

THE OLD ONE: I'm sorry.

THE MAN: Sorry? That's all right.

THE OLD ONE: You have to forgive me.

THE MAN: I have to?

THE OLD ONE: That's all I want.

THE MAN: Aha.

THE OLD ONE: I beg you. (SILENCE) Yes.

THE MAN: You could have asked for forgiveness before, If you really wanted it.

THE OLD ONE: Are you there? (REACHES OUT WITH HIS HAND.) Where are you?

THE MAN: I'm here. In the chair.

THE OLD ONE: Couldn't you . . .

THE MAN: What?

THE OLD ONE: Take my hand?

THE MAN: (AFTER HESITATING A LONG TIME, TAKES HIS HAND.) Yes, it's fine.

THE OLD ONE: What did you say?

THE MAN: It feels familiar.

THE OLD ONE: Yes . . .

(THE MAN TAKES HIS HAND BACK; THE OLD ONE LETS HIS HAND FALL DOWN AND GETS VERY STILL.)

(SILENCE)

THE MAN: Are you sleeping?

THE OLD ONE: Where is Emma?

THE MAN: Which Emma?

THE OLD ONE: Where's she?

THE MAN: How should I know?

THE OLD ONE: She sat in the garden with Ingrid and her brother.

THE MAN: Ingrid? Mom?

THE OLD ONE: She was so beautiful.

THE MAN: Mom?

THE OLD ONE: She had long dark hair . . . and she laughed . . . with her brother . . . in the hammock.

THE MAN: Mom didn't have dark hair. She was blond or grey. All grey, unless she colored it. (SILENCE) She had grey hair. (SILENCE. THE MAN STANDS UP, GOES OVER TO THE OLD ONE, LOOKS AT HIM, STANDS STILL FOR A WHILE, TURNS AROUND AND SITS DOWN AGAIN.)

THE DOCTOR: (FROM THE SCENE BEFORE, COMES IN.) Is someone here?

THE MAN: Yes.

THE DOCTOR: Sorry, I didn't know.

THE MAN: He's my old man.

THE DOCTOR: Aha.

THE MAN: I haven't seen him for five years. And now he died. He died right now.

THE DOCTOR: Right now?

THE MAN: Yes, a few minutes ago.

THE DOCTOR: Really.

THE MAN: We sat here talking and then he died.

THE DOCTOR: No, he died this morning.

THE MAN: This morning?

THE DOCTOR: Yes, around six this morning. He died. Right here. (WALKS OUT.)

■

(THE DOCTOR IS MEETING THE MOTHER OF THE DEAD GIRL, IN AN EXAMINATION ROOM WITH THE PREGNANT NURSE.)

THE PREGNANT NURSE: I'll see if someone is available.

THE DOCTOR: Do you have a minute?

THE PREGNANT NURSE: No.

THE DOCTOR: Why not?

THE PREGNANT NURSE: Because I don't.

THE DOCTOR: OK. Just wanted to tell you that I can't tonight.

THE PREGNANT NURSE: No.

THE DOCTOR: No, sorry.

THE PREGNANT NURSE: OK.

THE DOCTOR: I'm sorry, but it won't work out. Something came up. Something I have to deal with.

THE PREGNANT NURSE: Good. (GOES BACK INTO THE ROOM AND EMBRACES THE MOTHER OF THE GIRL.) Do you want to rest for a while? (THE MOTHER OF THE GIRL SHAKES HER HEAD.) I'm sure there'll be a doctor here soon.

THE MOTHER OF THE GIRL: Yes, thank you.

THE PREGNANT NURSE: Are you nauseous? (SILENCE) There's so much going on right now. Saturday night. It's like a war zone out there.

THE MOTHER OF THE GIRL: Are the policemen still here?

THE PREGNANT NURSE: Policemen?

THE MOTHER OF THE GIRL: They are waiting for me out there . . . Are they still here?

THE PREGNANT NURSE: I don't know.

THE MOTHER OF THE GIRL: She was so kind, the female officer. She has a little girl too, who is thirteen years old. Her name is Emma.

THE PREGNANT NURSE: Emma? Yes, it's quite a common name.

THE MOTHER OF THE GIRL: (STANDS UP) I have to get home. I have to be home.

THE PREGNANT NURSE: I'm sure it'll be quick.

THE MOTHER OF THE GIRL: She's all alone.

THE PREGNANT NURSE: Who?

THE MOTHER OF THE GIRL: Johanna. (PAUSE) They've found her. (SILENCE) She was in the little house on the playground where she used to play when she was little.

THE PREGNANT NURSE: Yes . . .

THE MOTHER OF THE GIRL: We were there all the time when she was little.

THE PREGNANT NURSE: Johanna?

THE MOTHER OF THE GIRL: We always used to play there. You could get coffee, and if it rained you could go into the barrack for shelter.

THE PREGNANT NURSE: Wait a second, I'll see if there's someone who can come in to see you. (WALKS OUT, MEETS HENRY.)

HENRY: Hello.

THE PREGNANT NURSE: No, you'll have to wait.

HENRY: No, I can't.

THE PREGNANT NURSE: Please wait a little while. Talk to the receptionist.

HENRY: I'm not sick.

THE PREGNANT NURSE: Please. Go to the window.

HENRY: No, I can't wait. I brought that woman here who's in the room you came from. In there. She's in there. She hasn't paid for the ride. The minister said he'd take care of it and now he's disappeared too and outside my cab is ticking money. Stop. (FOLLOWS THE PREGNANT NURSE.) Don't you hear what I'm saying?

THE PREGNANT NURSE: Please. You'll have to wait.

HENRY: How the hell can I wait? I'm losing money every fucking minute that's going to hell. It's my job we're talking about.

THE PREGNANT NURSE: I've got more important things right now. I don't have time.

HENRY: No, you don't have time. What am I to do then? I've got to get fucking paid for driving her here. I'm no fucking charity organization. I can't go to some fucking social service person if I don't have enough to live on. There isn't a single fucking person helping me.

(SILENCE)

HENRY: Fucking cunt.

THE PASTOR: (IS COMING UP THE CORRIDOR.) So sorry. Sorry.

HENRY Sorry?

THE PASTOR: I took a little longer than I thought.

HENRY: That's your job.

THE PASTOR: I had to make a phone call.

HENRY: I'm sorry.

THE PASTOR: So, how much do I owe you?

HENRY: How the hell would I know.

THE PASTOR: How much? How much do I owe you?

HENRY: How many customers do you think I've lost by now?

THE PASTOR: I guess a few customers.

HENRY: My God . . .

THE PASTOR: I'm sorry but this is all I'm carrying on me. I wasn't prepared to run out this quickly. It was unexpected. But it usually is. (SHORT PAUSE) All I can do is thank you for being patient.

HENRY: Aha.

THE PASTOR: She was completely distraught. I had her child in my bible studies class last spring. I remember her lovely, bright smile.

HENRY: What the hell am I to do?

THE PASTOR: (LOOKS AT HIS WATCH.) I'd better call my wife to bring our car to pick me up.

HENRY: Yea, why don't you. (LEAVES.)

∎

THE PASTOR: (IS RUNNING, BARE TORSO, IN A SUBURB THAT SEEMS TO HAVE SPRUNG UP FROM A FORMER INDUSTRIAL PARK. HE RUNS PAST A WOMAN, WHO IS SITTING ON A BENCH MADE OF STEEL. HE RUNS PAST HER TWICE. BOTH TIMES HE TURNS TO LOOK AT THE WOMAN WHILE RUNNING. THE THIRD TIME HE RUNS PAST HER A LITTLE SLOWER WHILE STARING AT HER, THEN STOPS, TURNS AROUND AND GOES BACK TO HER AND STANDS IN FRONT OF THE WOMAN WHO IS SMOKING.) Are you all alone? (SILENCE) Are you sitting here by yourself?

THE OTHER MOTHER: No.

THE PASTOR: Who's with you? (PAUSE) Are you waiting for someone?

THE OTHER MOTHER: Yes. My husband.

THE PASTOR: Your husband? Where is he?

THE OTHER MOTHER: He'll be here soon.

THE PASTOR: Yes, you shouldn't sit here alone.

THE OTHER MOTHER: You should just keep running.

THE PASTOR: Yes. (SILENCE) Are you interested in fellatio?

THE OTHER MOTHER: What?

THE PASTOR: Give me some oral sex? Is that something you might consider? That's the only thing that helps me. I have a problem with my nerves. I have insomnia. I've seen my doctor and he gave me medications, but I don't think I'm any better. Could you suck me off, please?

THE OTHER MOTHER: No, I can't.

THE PASTOR: Please, please. I think it would help me. Please help me. It would be so wonderful. Since we are the only ones here.

THE OTHER MOTHER: No. I don't want to.

THE PASTOR: I could pay you if that would . . . if that would make it easier for you.

THE OTHER MOTHER: Why don't you leave?

THE PASTOR: I just want you to give me a blow job. In the usual way. You must know what to do. These days every woman knows what to do. I guess they learn it in kindergarten. I don't know. I have no children. Unfortunately we didn't have any. However much we tried.

THE OTHER MOTHER: If you don't leave I'll call my husband.

THE PASTOR: I 'm not out to do evil.

THE OTHER MOTHER: Now I'm calling the Police. (TAKES OUT HER CELL PHONE.) I'm calling.

THE PASTOR: I just want some company.

THE OTHER MOTHER: Get away from here.

THE PASTOR: Closeness. That's all I'm asking for. Closeness. To be close to someone. Just for a little while. Since we're the only ones here. That's not so dangerous. I absolutely don't want to harm you in any way. On the contrary. Do you understand me? (SHORT PAUSE) Do you understand? (THE WIFE OF THE PASTOR IS COMING TOWARDS THEM CARRYING A HANDBAG AND DRESSED IN A SUIT.) Look, there's my wife, Ann-Mari. I forgot about her. She had to sit in the car waiting while I was talking to you. (SHORT PAUSE) Were you waiting for me, my dear?

THE WIFE OF THE PASTOR: Where did you go?

THE PASTOR: I started to talk to this woman. I don't know her name.

THE WIFE OF THE PASTOR: You were just going to . . .

THE PASTOR: I don't know your name. What's your name?

THE WIFE OF THE PASTOR: Where's your shirt and your jacket?

THE PASTOR: I don't think we introduced ourselves. Well, it doesn't matter.

THE WIFE OF THE PASTOR: Where are your clothes?

THE PASTOR: We're all humans.

THE OTHER MOTHER: He accosted me. (SILENCE) He came up and asked me to perform oral sex on him. (THE WIFE OF THE PASTOR IS STANDING PERFECTLY STILL.) He came up to me just like that and asked if I wanted to do it. I've called the police. (THE WIFE OF THE PASTOR IS VERY STILL AND QUIET.) They're sending a car right away, to the park.

THE WIFE OF THE PASTOR: Go and sit in the car. Go back to the car.

THE OTHER MOTHER: Fucking swine.

THE WIFE OF THE PASTOR: Why don't you go to the car?

THE PASTOR: Yes, I'm going. So sorry, I didn't want to cause any harm.

THE OTHER MOTHER: You're a fucking degenerate. Disgusting.

(THE PASTOR LEAVES.)

THE WIFE OF THE PASTOR: He's been depressed lately, not himself. He's been seeing a therapist, but I guess it takes a long time before you see some improvement.

THE OTHER MOTHER: That's something I shouldn't have to suffer for. I have enough at my work. (PAUSE) I wonder where they are? The cops. It was crawling with cops here just a couple of hours ago, when I was on my break. I guess they are at the station house playing cards. (SHORT PAUSE) I just came here for some peace and quiet and a cigarette. My whole body is shaking. (SHORT PAUSE) Suck him off? (SHORT PAUSE) Dream away, fucking idiot.

THE WIFE OF THE PASTOR: I don't understand anything. I don't know what's gotten into him.

THE OTHER MOTHER: No, doesn't look like they are going to show up. I guess they have more important things to do. Some football pool or something. (STANDS UP.) I don't give a damn about them. You don't get any help anyway in this fucking country that you've worked yourself to death for. No thanks at all. Anyone can come up to you and degrade you whenever they want to. I guess I'm not worth any better. I guess I look like I want to be degraded. He didn't even say hello. Just came up and asked if I wanted to have his old cock in my mouth. Why would I want that? And look, there's another one.

THE MAN: (IS WALKING UP TO THEM.) Hi, there.

THE OTHER MOTHER: And who the hell are you?

THE MAN: And who the hell are you?

THE OTHER MOTHER: I don't think I know you.

THE MAN: Go to hell. (LEAVES.)

■

THE MAN: (HE BUMPS INTO THE PREGNANT NURSE IN THE STAIRCASE OF THE APARTMENT HOUSE.) Hi. Hello.

THE PREGNANT NURSE: Hello, hello.

THE MAN: I guess you don't remember me.

THE PREGNANT NURSE: I think I do.

THE MAN: I used to live here before, but that was quite a while ago But now I'm living here again on the third floor.

THE PREGNANT NURSE: Yes, that's right. I hope you haven't heard anything?

THE MAN: I hear quite a lot.

THE PREGNANT NURSE: Are we too loud?

THE MAN: Not that I know.

THE PREGNANT NURSE: The walls are so thin here.

THE MAN: Yes.

THE PREGNANT NURSE: I was thinking that you might have heard something about the meeting. About the condo conversion.

THE MAN: Condo conversion?

THE PREGNANT NURSE: That's what they want to do.

THE MAN: I haven't heard shit about it.

THE PREGNANT NURSE: That it's going to happen. I guess it won't happen. People here don't have the money for it, even if it will be cheap.

THE MAN: Not me anyway.

THE PREGNANT NURSE: No, you'll never get away from here.

THE MAN: Not alive anyway.

THE PREGNANT NURSE: No.

THE MAN: Nothing to hope for.

THE PREGNANT NURSE: No. Silly to hope.

(SHORT PAUSE)

THE MAN: I have one more flight to go.

THE PREGNANT NURSE: I mean . . . (PUTS HER HAND ON HER STOMACH.)

THE MAN: Oh that, yes, well, see you around, I hope.

THE PREGNANT NURSE: Not out of the question.

THE MAN: I mean since I live here.

∎

THE MAN: (WALKS INTO HIS APARTMENT.) Yes, oh my God. (SILENCE) Anyone home? (SHORT PAUSE) Hello. (SILENCE) Why isn't she home now that she has no job? I could use a little company. (SHORT PAUSE) I have to leave soon again. (SILENCE) (WALKS OVER TO THE DOOR LEADING TO THE BOY'S ROOM. OPENS THE DOOR.) Are you there? (SILENCE) (WALKS UP TO THE BED WHERE THE BOY IS, TRIES TO PULL AWAY THE COMFORTER.) Why are you in bed in the middle of the day? (SHORT PAUSE) What are you doing? (SHORT PAUSE) Are you in bed jerking off?

THE BOY: Leave me alone.

THE MAN: What's wrong with you? (SILENCE) What the hell, answer me.

THE BOY: Get lost.

THE MAN: Shut up.

THE BOY: Leave me alone.

THE MAN: You don't speak to me like that. I'm your Dad. Do you get it? (SHORT PAUSE) Do you get that? (TAKES A HARD GRIP OF HIS FACE.) Get it? Do you get it or not? I am your dad. You have to behave. (SHORT PAUSE) What do you say?

THE BOY: Yes.

THE MAN: What? I don't hear anything.

THE BOY: Yea, yea.

THE MAN: Good. . . . Better shape up or you'll get it from me.

THE MOM: (COMES INTO THE APARTMENT.) Hello.

THE MAN: Here she is.

THE MOM: Where are you?

THE MAN: (GOES TO HER.) Where have you been?

THE MOM: You know, I went to the doctor.

THE MAN: Was that today?

THE MOM: Where's Rainer?

THE MAN: Rainer? Why don't you ask about me?

THE MOM: Where is he?

THE MAN: In there. In his room. Sulking.

THE MOM: Really.

THE MAN: I tried to talk to him, but you can't get a sensible word out of him. He's like a fucking animal. (SILENCE) I'm going out for a while.

THE MOM: You're going out?

THE MAN: Yes, I can't stand being here for too long.

THE MOM: I see.

THE MAN: Is that all you have to say?

THE MOM: I went to the doctor.

THE MAN: I know. You told me.

THE MOM: Yes.

THE MAN: What about it? (SHORT PAUSE) Are you sick?

THE MOM: No.

THE MAN: Well, then.

THE MOM: (QUIETLY) I'm pregnant. I'm going to have a baby.

(SILENCE)

THE MAN: You are, are you?

THE MOM: In my third month. It must have been the first time . . .

THE MAN: Yes, we were drunk then, drunk like swine. (THE DOORBELL RINGS.) Who could it be? (SHORT PAUSE) Aren't you going to open?

(THE MOM OPENS THE DOOR.)

THE WIFE OF THE PASTOR: (IN THE DOORWAY.) I'm sorry to disturb you . . .

THE MOM: What do you want?

THE WIFE OF THE PASTOR: I was supposed to see Mrs. Ardelius who lives across from you, your neighbor.

THE MAN: Yes, I know her. Doesn't she open the door?

THE WIFE OF THE PASTOR: It doesn't look like it. I've been ringing the bell for ten minutes.

THE MOM: I guess she's sleeping.

THE WIFE OF THE PASTOR: But there's no one opening the door.

THE MOM: Her son is usually at home.

THE WIFE OF THE PASTOR: Did you happen to see him today?

THE MOM: He never goes out. He's always at home. He gets visitors instead.

THE WIFE OF THE PASTOR: Aha.

THE MOM: Well, she should be home. Home services were here this morning and left food for her, since she can't walk the stairs. She hasn't been outside for years. Sometimes she sits on her balcony.

THE WIFE OF THE PASTOR: I guess I'll try later.

THE MOM: Hope nothing happened to her.

WIFE OF THE MINISTER: Yes, let's hope so. Thank you.

THE MOM: That's all right. (CLOSES THE DOOR.)

(THE WIFE OF THE PASTOR WALKS OVER TO THE NEIGHBOR'S DOOR AND STARTS TO KNOCK.)

■

THE OLD WOMAN: (OPENS THE DOOR.) What is it?

THE WIFE OF THE PASTOR: Well, hello. I'm here to see Benny. Is he here?

THE OLD WOMAN: I was sleeping. I was asleep. I was asleep in bed.

THE WIFE OF THE PASTOR: May I come in? I'm here to see Benny. I'm his probation officer, Ann-Marie. We've met before. (ENTERS THE ROOM, WHICH IS VERY SMALL AND DIRTY, VERY MESSY. THERE IS AN OLD COUCH BY THE WINDOW COVERED BY A BIG DIRTY BLANKET.) Where is he?

THE OLD WOMAN: Who?

THE WIFE OF THE PASTOR: Benny. He knew I was coming at three p.m. That had been decided. He didn't show up last Wednesday.

THE OLD WOMAN: I haven't seen him.

THE WIFE OF THE PASTOR: So, he isn't here?

THE OLD WOMAN: I don't know.

THE WIFE OF THE PASTOR: When did you see him last?

THE OLD WOMAN: Last? (SHORT PAUSE) I've been sleeping. It's the pills. The pills make me sleepy. I take . . . I think it is seventeen pills that I have to take. For the swelling.

THE WIFE OF THE PASTOR: Where is he? He's not allowed to not show up when we've made promises to each other. He knows that. Then he might be taken in again. He's just out on trial. To show that he's trying to manage on his own. I have to report this. Are there any more rooms?

THE OLD WOMAN: Rooms?

THE WIFE OF THE PASTOR: Could he be here somewhere else?

THE OLD WOMAN: I haven't seen him.

THE WIFE OF THE PASTOR: May I take a look? (GOES INTO ANOTHER ALMOST EMPTY ROOM.) Is this where he lives?

THE OLD WOMAN: Yes . . . who?

(THERE ARE SOUNDS COMING FROM A SMALL FREE-STANDING CLOSET BY ONE OF THE WALLS.)

THE WIFE OF THE PASTOR: Is that where he is? Benny? (SHORT PAUSE) It's Ann-Marie. We're supposed to see each other today, you and me (SHORT PAUSE) Come on out. Now I'm opening the door. (OPENS THE DOOR.)

BENNY: (A BIG NAKED MAN FALLS OUT OF THE CLOSET. THERE'S A ROPE AROUND HIS NECK.)

THE OLD WOMAN: I have to get some help with my teeth.

WIFE OF THE MINISTER: What did you do?

(BENNY IS ON THE FLOOR ROCKING BACK AND FORTH.)

THE WIFE OF THE PASTOR: (IS LOOKING AT HIM.) Stop doing that.

BENNY: I want to die. I want to die. I'm dead.

THE WIFE OF THE PASTOR: Yes, yes . . .

THE OLD WOMAN: What's going on?

BENNY: Mom, I love you. I love you. I love those who pick me up. I don't want to go back.

THE WIFE OF THE PASTOR: We can't have it like this. You understand, don't you?

BENNY: I love you, Mom. (THE OLD WOMAN STARTS TO LAUGH.) Yes, you're right. We have fun here, you and I.

THE WIFE OF THE PASTOR: I've got to call the cops.

BENNY: No. I don't want to go back. I want to die. Let me die. Why don't you let me die?

THE WIFE OF THE PASTOR: Do you have a telephone? I forgot my cell phone.

THE OLD WOMAN: Cell phone?

BENNY: I didn't do anything. I didn't do anything. I haven't done shit. I wasn't there.

THE WIFE OF THE PASTOR: My cell phone. I forgot to bring it. I don't know where I put it. Is there a phone I can use somewhere?

BENNY: They stole mine. There were some fucking criminals who robbed me when I went out to buy candy. They threatened me with a knife, and stole my phone. Those assholes. After that I haven't dared to go out.

THE OLD WOMAN: Stop laughing.

BENNY: I'm not laughing. You're the one laughing.

THE OLD WOMAN: Stop it, I said. I need a smoke. Where are my cigarettes?

THE WIFE OF THE PASTOR: I'll ask your neighbor. Stay here. You can't go anywhere.

THE OLD WOMAN: Did you take my last cigarettes? (KICKS BENNY.) Did you smoke my last cigarette, you fucking bastard?

(THE WIFE OF THE PASTOR KNOCKS ON THE DOOR OF "THE MOM" AGAIN.)

THE MAN: (OPENS THE DOOR.) Did she let you in?

THE WIFE OF THE PASTOR: May I borrow your phone? I have to make an important phone call. I happened to misplace my cell phone.

THE MOM: Of course. Please, right here. I hope nothing has happened.

THE WIFE OF THE PASTOR: Thank you. (TAKES THE PHONE.) It's confidential.

THE MOM: What is it?

THE WIFE OF THE PASTOR: The phone call. It's . . . private.

THE MOM: Yes, of course. Sure. I won't listen. (GOES INTO THE LIVING ROOM AND SITS DOWN ON THE COUCH, WAITING. HEARS WHEN THE PHONE CALL IS OVER AND WHEN THE FRONT DOOR CLOSES.) At least she could've said "thank you." Not too much to ask for. (IS SITTING STILL. STANDS UP AND GOES TO THE DOOR LEADING TO THE BOY'S ROOM. OPENS IT.) Are you there? Rainer? (SILENCE) What are you doing? (GOES OVER TO THE BED. TRIES TO REMOVE THE COMFORTER.) Are you sleeping?

THE BOY: Leave me alone.

THE MOM: What's wrong? (SHORT PAUSE) Rainer? (SILENCE) Answer me.

THE BOY: No.

THE MOM: Don't you feel well?

THE BOY: I want to be left alone.

THE MOM: Yes, I'll leave you alone. (LOOKS AT HER HAND, WHICH SEEMS TO BE WET.) Are you crying? (SHORT PAUSE) Why are you bawling?

THE BOY: I'm not bawling.

THE MOM: Your face is all wet.

THE BOY: Get out.

THE MOM: Yes, but . . . did something happen in school today?

THE BOY: What the hell. (SITS UP.)

THE MOM: Rainer, what's wrong?

THE BOY: Leave me alone.

THE MOM: Sure . . . but I want to talk to you. (SILENCE) It's important.

THE BOY: Not to me.

THE MOM: Yes it is, for you too.

THE BOY: Why can't you leave me alone? (SILENCE) What?

THE MOM: Well . . .

THE BOY: You said it was important.

THE MOM: Yes, I guess it is . . . it's about Arvid.

THE BOY: Who?

THE MOM: Arvid.

THE BOY: Oh, him?

THE MOM: Yes. Arvid . . . your dad.

THE BOY: He's not.

THE MOM: What did you say?

THE BOY: He isn't my dad.

THE MOM: Sure he is.

THE BOY: No, he isn't.

THE MOM: What are you talking about?

THE BOY: I don't have one.

THE MOM: Of course you do. He's out there.

THE BOY: I don't give a damn about him.

THE MOM: Really. (SILENCE) Well, we've been talking and now it's decided . . . that he's going to live with us again, that we'll become a family again. It won't be the way it was before. He's a lot calmer these days. Now he has a good job and he goes to AA meetings once a week. Every Thursday night. He's really going to try. He's not just saying that. I need his help; we need it. I have no job and my severance pay ends this month and then we won't have a cent to live on. And I can't manage to take care of both you and Sanna. I need someone to help me. Otherwise I don't know what will happen. We might have to move out, and where would we go?

THE BOY: If he's here I'm moving out.

THE MOM: Move where?

THE BOY: Away from here.

THE MOM: Where? Where would you go?

THE BOY: It's none of your business, you fucking whore.

THE MOM: What are you saying?

THE BOY: It's because of him that Sanna is in the nut house.

THE MOM: She's not in the nut house. She is in a psychiatric clinic.

THE BOY: Because of what he did to her.

THE MOM: He didn't do anything.

THE BOY: That's why she's sick, why she'll never get any better.

THE MOM: I would've known, I would have noticed something.

THE BOY: You did, you did too, fucking whore. (RUNS OUT THE FRONT DOOR AND BUMPS INTO THE NEIGHBOR.)

THE NEIGHBOR: Take it easy. Look where you're fucking going.

THE BOY: Shut up.

THE NEIGHBOR: Shut up?

THE BOY: Fucking idiot.

THE NEIGHBOR: (GRABS THE BOY.) What the hell are you saying?

THE BOY: Let go of me.

THE NEIGHBOR: Don't you like it?

THE BOY: Let go of me, fucking asshole.

THE NEIGHBOR: I'm telling you, I'll let go when I want to.

THE BOY: Let go of me, fucking son of a bitch.

THE NEIGHBOR: (HITS HIM HARD, CONTINUES TO HIT HIM, SUDDENLY UNDERSTANDS WHAT HE IS DOING AND LETS GO OF HIM. THE BOY IS STILL ON THE GROUND.) Get up. Get up, I said. (SILENCE) So, get up. It was your own fault. You've only yourself to blame. (SHORT PAUSE) Come on, get up. You get what you ask for in this world. (WALKS AWAY.)

■

THE NEIGHBOR'S WIFE: (IS STANDING IN THE LIVING ROOM, IN THE LIGHT.) Hello. . . . Are you home?

THE NEIGHBOR: Yes, I'm home.

(SILENCE)

THE NEIGHBOR'S WIFE: Did something happen?

THE NEIGHBOR: No. (SHORT PAUSE) Why do you ask?

THE NEIGHBOR'S WIFE: No.

THE NEIGHBOR: I'm just a little tired.

(SILENCE)

THE NEIGHBOR'S WIFE: How are you?

THE NEIGHBOR: Fine. (GOES AND PUTS THE SHOPPING BAGS DOWN.)

THE NEIGHBOR'S WIFE: Erik?

THE NEIGHBOR: Yes?

(SILENCE)

THE NEIGHBOR'S WIFE: Did something happen?

THE NEIGHBOR: No, nothing.

THE NEIGHBOR'S WIFE: Sure?

THE NEIGHBOR: Sure.

THE NEIGHBOR'S WIFE: OK.

THE NEIGHBOR: Absolutely. . . . I'm just a little tired.

THE NEIGHBOR'S WIFE: Yes, I understand.

THE NEIGHBOR: I guess you are, too.

(SILENCE)

THE NEIGHBOR'S WIFE: How was work today?

THE NEIGHBOR: As usual. Nothing special.

THE NEIGHBOR'S WIFE: Why don't you tell me?

THE NEIGHBOR: What? (SHORT PAUSE) What do you want me to tell you?

THE NEIGHBOR'S WIFE: What you do.

THE NEIGHBOR: What I do? You know what I do.

THE NEIGHBOR'S WIFE: No, not really.

THE NEIGHBOR: I go to work and then I'm with you. That's what I do. Not much to talk about.

THE NEIGHBOR'S WIFE: Please talk to me . . . tell me . . . tell me about your work.

THE NEIGHBOR: My work? There's nothing to say about it. I do the same thing every day . . . same thing I've done for the last nine years. I'd rather forget about it. I don't want to have to talk about it, since I'm trying to forget about it when I'm not working. Now I'm going to put away what I bought . . . in the fridge.

THE NEIGHBOR'S WIFE: You don't talk enough . . .

THE NEIGHBOR: I don't . . . about what?

THE NEIGHBOR'S WIFE: About all kinds of things . . .what you're thinking . . . about this . . . how things are with you.

THE NEIGHBOR: You know how things are. I see people who don't have the strength to live any longer. Day in and day out they ask for help that doesn't exist.

THE NEIGHBOR'S WIFE: I didn't mean it as a criticism. It's just that . . .

THE NEIGHBOR: No, I understand.

THE NEIGHBOR'S WIFE: But you should also be able to talk to . . .

THE NEIGHBOR: That's fine. I know. That's what everybody says. (SHORT PAUSE) But it doesn't help. (SILENCE) It doesn't make you feel any better. (SILENCE)

THE NEIGHBOR'S WIFE: What did you get?

THE NEIGHBOR: Thai food. That's what you wanted, right?

THE NEIGHBOR'S WIFE: Thai food?

THE NEIGHBOR: Yes.

THE NEIGHBOR'S WIFE: Maybe. I don't remember . . . what I wanted. So, that's what smells.

THE NEIGHBOR: Yes, that's what you wanted.

THE NEIGHBOR'S WIFE: Today?

THE NEIGHBOR: Yes, that's what you said. That's why I got it.

THE NEIGHBOR'S WIFE: I don't know if I can eat it. I can't even stand the smell of it.

THE NEIGHBOR: No?

THE NEIGHBOR'S WIFE: There's no use eating when you vomit it all up anyway.

THE NEIGHBOR: You don't have to have it. It's just that you said that you were longing for it. Thai food.

THE NEIGHBOR'S WIFE: Did I say that? I'm sorry. I'm so difficult.

THE NEIGHBOR: Do you want something else?

THE NEIGHBOR'S WIFE: No, I can't even swallow food . . . but you have to eat.

THE NEIGHBOR: I can wait.

THE NEIGHBOR'S WIFE: Did you go all the way over to . . .

THE NEIGHBOR: Yes, you said you wanted . . . and that was the best, over there . . .

THE NEIGHBOR'S WIFE: Yes, I'm just causing problems—and now I'm going to die too. (SILENCE) I've got to joke around a little sometimes. (SHORT PAUSE) Do you want me to warm it up? (WALKS BEHIND HIM, PUTS HER HAND ON HIS CHEEK.) Should I start the oven?

THE NEIGHBOR: No, I'll wait a while. I told you I'd wait a while.

THE NEIGHBOR'S WIFE: (TRIES TO HUG HIM.) Couldn't you . . .

THE NEIGHBOR: I'm so cold.

THE NEIGHBOR'S WIFE: You are? I'm not.

THE NEIGHBOR: It's cold out there. The weather is fucking horrible.

THE NEIGHBOR'S WIFE: (ALMOST IRONICALLY) Yes, when, oh when, will we have summer?

THE NEIGHBOR: Summer? This is January.

THE NEIGHBOR'S WIFE: It is? Yes, of course it is. (SHORT PAUSE) Yes, hard to believe. (SILENCE) It looks so empty here.

THE NEIGHBOR: So, what did you do?

THE NEIGHBOR'S WIFE: What did I do?

THE NEIGHBOR: Yes. While I was gone.

THE NEIGHBOR'S WIFE: Yes, what did I do? (SHORT PAUSE) I defrosted the freezer. That's what I did . . . and I looked at old photographs.

THE NEIGHBOR: You did? That's good.

THE NEIGHBOR'S WIFE: It really needed it. (OPENS THE FREEZER.) Look how good it looks.

THE NEIGHBOR: Yes. Very good.

THE NEIGHBOR'S WIFE: Aren't you impressed?

THE NEIGHBOR: Sure I am.

THE NEIGHBOR'S WIFE: I put the berries and the mushrooms we picked last year on the top shelf, and then you have the vegetables and meat and fish and desserts in the three compartments below for you to use when you get hungry.

THE NEIGHBOR: Yes, that's good.

(SILENCE)

THE NEIGHBOR: Lena.

THE NEIGHBOR'S WIFE: I threw out some of the old stuff. A lot of it, really.

THE NEIGHBOR: Take off that fucking wig! Take it off, I said.

THE NEIGHBOR'S WIFE: No, that's . . .

THE NEIGHBOR: What the hell, why don't you take it off! It makes you look so ridiculous!

THE NEIGHBOR'S WIFE: Ridiculous?

THE NEIGHBOR: Yes, ridiculous. Silly. You look like a joke. Take it off. Take it off. Take it off. (SILENCE) I can't stand looking at it.

THE NEIGHBOR'S WIFE: I see.

(SILENCE)

THE NEIGHBOR: Sorry. I'm so sorry.

(SILENCE)

THE NEIGHBOR: I'm sorry.

THE NEIGHBOR'S WIFE: (LEAVES.)

THE NEIGHBOR: No, don't go. (SHORT PAUSE) Stay here. Don't go.

■

THE YOUNG WOMAN: Where am I?

THE NEIGHBOR: You are in the emergency room.

(SILENCE)

THE YOUNG WOMAN: Emergency room?

THE NEIGHBOR: Yes. In the psychiatric ward.

(SILENCE)

THE YOUNG WOMAN: I am?

THE NEIGHBOR: Yes. (SHORT PAUSE) You're alive.

THE YOUNG WOMAN: I am?

THE NEIGHBOR: Yes, you are.

THE YOUNG WOMAN: I'm alive?

THE NEIGHBOR: Yes. (SHORT PAUSE) Maybe it wasn't meant to be.

(SILENCE)

THE YOUNG WOMAN: No.

THE NEIGHBOR: Because you came here in time.

(SILENCE)

THE YOUNG WOMAN: Yes, sorry . . .

THE NEIGHBOR: Sorry?

THE YOUNG WOMAN: Yes.

(SILENCE)

THE NEIGHBOR: How are you?

THE YOUNG WOMAN: How I am?

THE NEIGHBOR: Yes.

THE YOUNG WOMAN: I don't know.

THE NEIGHBOR: Do you remember what happened?

THE YOUNG WOMAN: No, I . . .

THE NEIGHBOR: What did you say?

THE YOUNG WOMAN: No, I don't remember . . . I don't remember anything.

THE NEIGHBOR: I guess that's good. (SILENCE) I work here.

THE YOUNG WOMAN: Aha.

THE NEIGHBOR: I was here when you came in during the night.

THE YOUNG WOMAN: I came in?

THE NEIGHBOR: You came in around three in the morning.

THE YOUNG WOMAN: Is it still night?

THE NEIGHBOR: No, it's morning. (SILENCE) They pumped your stomach. It went well.

THE YOUNG WOMAN: Really.

THE NEIGHBOR: You'll probably feel a little pain in your throat for a couple of days, from the tube, but that's about it. I'm afraid we can't do much about what else is going on. (SILENCE) How do you feel?

THE YOUNG WOMAN: But . . . (SILENCE) Was I alone?

THE NEIGHBOR: Alone?

THE YOUNG WOMAN: When I came in?

THE NEIGHBOR: No, you weren't alone.

THE YOUNG WOMAN: No?

THE NEIGHBOR: There was a boy who came with you.

THE YOUNG WOMAN: Who?

THE NEIGHBOR: I don't know. That I don't know. I don't know who it was. (SILENCE) You'd better rest for a while.

THE YOUNG WOMAN: What time is it? (TRIES TO SIT UP.)

THE NEIGHBOR: No, lie down.

THE YOUNG WOMAN: What time is it?

THE NEIGHBOR: Almost eleven.

THE YOUNG WOMAN: Eleven? (SHORT PAUSE) In the night?

THE NEIGHBOR: No, it's morning. Eleven in the morning. That's what I said.

THE YOUNG WOMAN: That early?

THE NEIGHBOR: Yes.

(SILENCE)

THE YOUNG WOMAN: I don't know what I'm . . .

THE NEIGHBOR: No. (SHORT PAUSE) One never knows. (SILENCE) There are those who want to live . . . who don't want to die. Who aren't allowed to live. That's how it is. (SILENCE) Yes, there are those who really want to live, who have something to live for, but they aren't allowed, however much they want to . . . who don't give up . . . but who . . .

THE YOUNG WOMAN: Yes.

THE NEIGHBOR: Yes, this time it worked out. You woke up, didn't you?

THE YOUNG WOMAN: I'm trying . . . I'm trying . . .

THE NEIGHBOR: Yes, we try.

THE YOUNG WOMAN: I've tried . . .

THE NEIGHBOR: Soon you'll see a therapist.

THE YOUNG WOMAN: A therapist?

THE NEIGHBOR: Someone you can talk to.

THE YOUNG WOMAN: I don't want to talk.

THE NEIGHBOR: No harm in talking to someone.

THE YOUNG WOMAN: I don't want to talk any more.

(A DOOR OPENS.)

THE YOUNG WOMAN: I don't want to talk to anyone. I don't want to.

THE NEIGHBOR: Yes?

THE FRIEND: I don't know if I'm in . . . they said that she was here . . . Laura.

THE NEIGHBOR: Are you two related?

THE FRIEND: Yes, no, we're not. I'm just her boyfriend. Former boyfriend. We lived together. Us two.

THE NEIGHBOR: Aha.

THE FRIEND: We used to live together.

THE NEIGHBOR: I see.

THE FRIEND: How is she? How are things with her?

THE NEIGHBOR: She just woke up.

THE FRIEND: OK. (THE YOUNG WOMAN LOOKS AT HIM.) Yes, hello there, it's me. (SILENCE) How are you?

THE YOUNG WOMAN: Were you here last night?

THE FRIEND: Here? Last night? No. We were celebrating.

THE YOUNG WOMAN: With whom? Who were you with?

THE FRIEND: My sister, Tanja.

THE YOUNG WOMAN: So, who brought me here then?

THE FRIEND: Was someone here? Who?

THE NEIGHBOR: I think it was your brother.

THE FRIEND: Yes, he called me this morning. He told me that she was here. I didn't know anything. I was celebrating my sister's birthday.
THE NEIGHBOR: Now try to rest a little. Someone else will be here soon. (LEAVES.)

THE FRIEND: Who was that?

THE YOUNG WOMAN: I don't know.

THE FRIEND: You don't know?

THE YOUNG WOMAN: He was here.

THE FRIEND: Can I sit here? (SILENCE) What the fuck did you do? (SHORT PAUSE) Hey? (SILENCE) What's wrong with you? (SILENCE) Hey, you. (SILENCE) . . . Look at me.

THE YOUNG WOMAN: I want to sleep.

THE FRIEND: Sleep?

THE YOUNG WOMAN: Yes.

THE FRIEND: Didn't you sleep enough? (SILENCE) What kind of pills were they? How many did you take?

THE YOUNG WOMAN: I didn't count them.

THE FRIEND: Maybe you should've. (SILENCE) Your breast is showing. (SILENCE) You fucking scared me to death.

THE YOUNG WOMAN: Really. Good.

THE FRIEND: Don't you get it? When you do something like that.

(SILENCE)

THE YOUNG WOMAN: I called you. You hung up on me.

THE FRIEND: What the hell was I supposed to do?

THE YOUNG WOMAN: You turned off your cell phone.

THE FRIEND: I was with my sister, who had just been through an operation for a brain tumor, and had just gotten out of the hospital and needed to do some fun stuff with her children and her friends, and I don't have the strength to constantly talk about our relationship. I can't. I can't do it anymore.

THE YOUNG WOMAN: You just shut me off . . . just cut me out.

THE FRIEND: What the hell am I supposed to do?

THE YOUNG WOMAN: I can't take it . . .when you shut me off . . . and don't answer.

THE FRIEND: What am I supposed to do? Tell me.

THE YOUNG WOMAN: I don't know.

THE FRIEND: Me neither. (SHORT PAUSE) I have to have my own life. We aren't even living together anymore. I moved out, didn't I? I'm living with Bjorn now. (SILENCE) Do you think I could get coffee somewhere? (SHORT PAUSE) Is there some fucking automat somewhere? I think I'm a little "hung over." Not that I drank that much . . . (SILENCE) Hey. Do you want something?

THE YOUNG WOMAN: Did you meet someone?

THE FRIEND: What do you mean?

THE YOUNG WOMAN: Did you meet someone?

THE FRIEND: Who?

THE YOUNG WOMAN: Someone you slept with?

THE FRIEND: No, I did not.

(SILENCE)

THE YOUNG WOMAN: You're lying.

THE FRIEND: Really.

THE YOUNG WOMAN: I know you're lying. You brought someone.

THE FRIEND: I did? Who the hell did I bring?

THE YOUNG WOMAN: Stina.

THE FRIEND: Stina? (SHORT PAUSE) Which Stina?

THE YOUNG WOMAN: I know. (SHORT PAUSE) I know everything.

THE FRIEND: Really. (SHORT PAUSE) You do?

THE YOUNG WOMAN: She told me herself. She's told me everything. You want to have a little kid with her. With that whore.

■

THE FRIEND: But, my God . . .

THE OTHER ONE: What's going on?

THE FRIEND: Well, sorry.

THE OTHER ONE: I guess you'll have to wait your fucking turn. Don't you see that I'm standing here?

THE FRIEND: I just wanted a cup of coffee.

THE OTHER ONE: So? That's what I'm getting.

THE FRIEND: Yea, sorry.

THE OTHER ONE: Didn't you see me standing here?

THE FRIEND: That's OK.

THE OTHER ONE: What's OK?

THE FRIEND: No, nothing.

THE OTHER ONE: No.

THE FRIEND: I'm sorry.

THE OTHER ONE: That's better.

THE FRIEND: (GETS HIS CUP OF COFFEE AND SITS DOWN, AS DOES THE OTHER ONE.) You're doing a good job here. The place looks good. (SILENCE) I've read a lot about how bad the hygiene . . . the cleanliness is in hospitals nowadays.

THE OTHER ONE: Not here anyway. You've never read that.

THE FRIEND: No, no, I can see that.

(SHORT PAUSE)

THE OTHER ONE: We've never had any complaints.

THE FRIEND: No, that's . . . that's what I mean.

THE OTHER ONE: We've been cleaning here for three years without a single complaint.

THE FRIEND: That's really . . . so, that's your job?

THE OTHER ONE: Yes, seems that way. (SHORT PAUSE) Until I start my military training . . . in three years.

THE FRIEND: Three years? Really?

THE OTHER ONE: In Serbia.

THE FRIEND: Oh, there.

(SILENCE)

THE OTHER ONE: I guess it's a job like any other job. You either do a good job or not.

THE FRIEND: I guess.

THE OTHER ONE: You see a lot of weird stuff here.

THE FRIEND: I bet you do.

THE OTHER ONE: Lucky for me I have my faith.

THE FRIEND: Yea, I guess . . . Are you finished?

THE OTHER ONE: No, next year. Then I'm going back home.

THE FRIEND: No, I mean for today.

THE OTHER ONE: No, I'm done for today.

(SILENCE)

THE OTHER ONE: Last night I was cleaning a room with a young chick lying there who had died, had committed suicide . . . cleaned floor and toilet, but of course, that room has to be clean as well. No one had come to see her. No parents. No one. Just she herself. Don't know how old she was, eighteen, maybe nineteen.

THE FRIEND: Really.

THE OTHER ONE: God decides when you're supposed to die. But it's really sad when someone that young dies.

THE FRIEND: Yes, there are . . . there are many who . . . who die these days.

THE OTHER ONE: Yes, I prayed. I prayed for her.

THE FRIEND: Aha.

THE OTHER ONE: I felt that God was there. In the room. With her. He had to be. Of course I had to clean the room. The smell was awful. Horrible.

THE FRIEND: (HIS CELL PHONE RINGS.) Who the hell . . . (TAPS IT.) Yes. Who is it? (SHORT PAUSE) Yes. Yes, that's me. No, I'm at the hospital. No. Just something that happened. (SHORT PAUSE) They have? How? (SHORT PAUSE) I know. But I don't have that cell phone. They stole it. No, I came home and they were gone, both of them. Someone stole them. I couldn't call. (SHORT PAUSE) What? (SHORT PAUSE) Heroin? (SHORT PAUSE) Not heroin. It was bicarbonate. Fucking old dried up bicarbonate. Not heroin. They're crazy. (SHORT PAUSE) I know. Sure. Yes. Sure. Sure, OK. (SHORT PAUSE) When? OK. (SHORT PAUSE) At nine? In the morning? Sure. Absolutely. (TURNS OFF THE CELL PHONE.) Fuck. (SHORT PAUSE) My lawyer. Why is he calling me? I have no cell phone. I told him it was stolen, the one I had and the other one. He said that they had found anthrax and heroin under the seat in my car. But it isn't my fucking car. It's my cousin's car. I'd just borrowed it to move a few things. Now they found heroin in it. What the hell can I do about that? All I have would be prescription stuff. Nothing else. I'm clean. I was working on a construction job a while back and I was moving some aluminum tubes when the cops stopped me. I was just picking up what was left and moving it to a different place. That was all. Then I was going to borrow it to pick up my kid. Liza. Maybe drive somewhere. But I couldn't pick her up today because something else came up. So I couldn't pick her up. And now my former girl friend has complained to the court and wants sole custody of the kid.

THE OTHER ONE: The kid?

THE FRIEND: My kid.

THE OTHER ONE: Girl?

THE FRIEND: Who?

THE OTHER ONE: Her?

THE FRIEND: Sure, sure she's a girl.

THE OTHER ONE: Old?

THE FRIEND: Old? No, five years old.

THE OTHER ONE: Young.

THE FRIEND: Yes, five, soon.

THE OTHER ONE: Cute?

THE FRIEND: Yes, unbelievably cute.

THE OTHER ONE: That's nice.

THE FRIEND: Yes, but I hardly ever get to see her . . . the last time was at her birthday party when she turned four with balloons and cake. Otherwise they make a hell of a big deal just because I missed picking her up a few times when I've had other important things to do. What the hell am I to do?

THE OTHER ONE: I know.

THE FRIEND: If there's someone who's fucking up here it's her. But they don't believe me. The social services . . . you know . . . the . . . the ones who make the decisions like over life and death, they don't believe me. What the fuck are they called? Those fucking secretaries?

■

("THE OTHER ONE" OPENS A DOOR TO AN APARTMENT, STOPS, LOOKS INTO IT. THE ROOM IS PRACTICALLY EMPTY OF FURNITURE EXCEPT FOR A BIG, OLD, LOW COUCH AND A TV AND A COUPLE OF SIMPLE CHAIRS.)

THE OLDER FATHER: (AROUND SIXTY, BIG, HALF-DRESSED, HIS ARM AROUND A YOUNG WOMAN WHO IS HIS DAUGHTER, AROUND EIGHTEEN, TWENTY YEARS OLD. SHE IS DRESSED IN A SHORT SKIRT, STOCKINGS WITH RUNS IN THEM, A THIN UNDERSHIRT, HEAVILY MADE UP.) Do you think you're living in some fucking fleabag motel where you can come and go as you please instead of a good, stable home?

THE YOUNG DAUGHTER: Ouch, you're hurting me.

THE OLDER FATHER: You're supposed to be home at eleven, and not a minute later, when you're allowed to go out.

THE YOUNG DAUGHTER: Let go of me. Let go, I said.

THE OLDER FATHER: If you aren't home by eleven, as I've told you to, you might as well sleep in the street like a fucking whore. How the hell do you have the nerve to show up this late? Four o'clock in the morning? Do you know what you're doing?

THE YOUNG DAUGHTER: Daddy . . .

THE OLDER FATHER: Where the hell have you been?

THE YOUNG DAUGHTER: Just out.

THE OLDER FATHER: Out, yes . . . with whom?

THE YOUNG DAUGHTER: With my friends.

THE OLDER FATHER: Friends? What's that? In those clothes? Like a whore. You're hardly wearing anything on your body. You're fucking naked, showing everything. Everything you have.

THE YOUNG DAUGHTER: No.

THE OLDER FATHER: Where were you?

THE YOUNG DAUGHTER: Just at someone's house.

THE OLDER FATHER: Answer me. Whose house?

THE YOUNG DAUGHTER: Someone I know. We were celebrating. We had a wedding shower for her.

THE OLDER FATHER: What are you talking about?

THE YOUNG DAUGHTER: A party for someone who's getting married. We celebrated. At Tana's place and then I came home. She's getting married next Saturday.

THE OLDER FATHER: Did you even look at yourself?

THE YOUNG DAUGHTER: What?

THE OLDER FATHER: You look like a whore. Showing everything. Like a real whore.

THE YOUNG DAUGHTER: That's just for fun.

THE OLDER FATHER: Fun? To be a whore? Is that fun?

THE YOUNG DAUGHTER: No.

THE OLDER FATHER: Look at the Virgin Mary. Look at her. Look at how she looks down at you. Is that any fun?

(THE OTHER ONE IS STANDING BY THE DOOR, ABOUT TO LEAVE.)

THE OLDER FATHER: (WAIVES FOR HIM TO COME IN.) Come in. Come in. Come in and look at your sister the whore.

THE YOUNG DAUGHTER: I'm no whore. It's a costume for the party.

THE OLDER FATHER: Like a little whore.

THE YOUNG DAUGHTER: No.

THE OLDER FATHER: Are you a whore?

THE YOUNG DAUGHTER: No, I'm no whore.

THE OLDER FATHER: A whore. A real little whore with a shaved cunt. (HITS HER, PUSHES HER DOWN ON THE COUCH. SHE IS TRYING TO GET AWAY FROM HIS GRIP.) You little cunt. Show it. Show us your cunt. (GRABS HOLD OF "THE OTHER ONE" AND PULLS HIM TO THE COUCH.) Come here and look. (THE YOUNG DAUGHTER TRIES AGAIN TO GET AWAY; THE OLDER FATHER HITS HER IN A VERY BRUTAL WAY) Now, show him your cunt.

THE YOUNG DAUGHTER: No. Stop it.

THE OLDER FATHER: No way. (PULLS HER SKIRT UP.) Lie still you little fucking whore and show him what you have. If you can show your cunt to others you can show it to him, your own brother.

THE YOUNG DAUGHTER: Daddy!

THE OLDER FATHER: He hasn't seen that many. Let him have some fun.

THE YOUNG DAUGHTER: No.

THE OLDER FATHER: (OPENS UP HER LEGS, THEN PUSHES THE OTHER ONE'S HEAD DOWN INTO HER CROTCH.) Give her a lick. Why don't you lick her fucking cunt. Why shouldn't we have some pleasure from this fucking whore. Lick her and put your tongue in. That's what she wants. Just like her fucking whore of a mother. They are made of the same rotten stuff. Same shit. Same rotten shit. (THE YOUNG DAUGHTER SCREAMS.) Just you wait. You'll soon have something to scream about. Wait and I'll give you something that'll make you scream. Keep screaming. Soon you won't scream anymore. I'll get you screaming, you little cunt.

THE YOUNG DAUGHTER: Mommy.

THE OLDER FATHER: Mommy?

THE YOUNG DAUGHTER: Mommy . . .

THE OLDER FATHER: She should see you now.

■

THE OLDER MOTHER: (IS SITTING IN A SMALL ROOM WITH JUST TWO CHAIRS AND A TABLE. THE OLDEST SON IS SITTING ACROSS FROM HER.) How are you?

THE OLDEST SON: I guess I'm OK.

THE OLDER MOTHER: Are You?

THE OLDEST SON: Yes, what can I say? I'm OK.

(SILENCE)

THE OLDER MOTHER: You seem bigger.

THE OLDEST SON: Bigger?

THE OLDER MOTHER: Your shoulders, your chest . . . the arms. They seem bigger.

THE OLDEST SON: The work out. I work out here.

THE OLDER MOTHER: Your neck too. Is it stronger too?

THE OLDEST SON: That's all there is to do here. Work out. Work out and . . . and then work out even more.

THE OLDER MOTHER: I hardly recognize you.

THE OLDEST SON: No. You have to do something.

THE OLDER MOTHER: I guess . . .

THE OLDEST SON: Yes, what else could I do? (SILENCE) I don't want you to come here.

THE OLDER MOTHER: No . . .

THE OLDEST SON: It's not good for me. It makes it more difficult. It's easier when you never see anyone. Then you don't . . . you don't have to think about how it is on the outside while you're here. Then the days just go by.

THE OLDER MOTHER: Yes . . . but I have to see you.

THE OLDEST SON: Then you don't have to care. You're all alone. That's better.

THE OLDER MOTHER: You mean I can't see you?

THE OLDEST SON: Yes, but it's . . .

THE OLDER MOTHER: You're in here for seven years.

THE OLDEST SON: Yes, but it'll go very fast, maybe.

THE OLDER MOTHER: No, not for me. Not for me.

THE OLDEST SON: Well, no use talking about it. It is what it is. Done is done. It's a fact.

(SILENCE)

THE OLDER MOTHER: Later you'll get out on leave, I guess.

THE OLDEST SON: Yes, in a few years. A couple of hours every third month maybe.

THE OLDER MOTHER: Yes.

THE OLDEST SON: In this neighborhood . . . go to a pizza place, or . . . I don't know.

(SILENCE)

THE OLDER MOTHER: So, what are you doing?

THE OLDEST SON: Right now? I work out. I told you. (SHORT PAUSE) I guess that I'll study, chemistry, when I have the time. I've put in an application for the books . . . I'll need.

(SILENCE)

THE OLDER MOTHER: I left some clothes with the guard, in case you . . .

THE OLDEST SON: No, I get clothes here. I get everything here. Like these.

(SILENCE)

THE OLDER MOTHER: Isn't there anything you want?

THE OLDEST SON: Yea. (SHORT PAUSE) It wouldn't be so bad being back home again, to be sitting in the sun in the big square drinking the best espresso in the world. To catch a soccer match, or go to Dinara to see Grandpa. Lijepa nasa domovino.

THE OLDER MOTHER: Yes, that's what they say. It won't work. We'll never be able to go back again.

THE OLDEST SON: Don't say that . . . How's Ivo?

THE OLDER MOTHER: I don't know. Since he's living with your dad.

THE OLDEST SON: And how's he?

THE OLDER MOTHER: He doesn't want to see me. It's been many years. I don't know how anyone is. (SILENCE) That's why I don't want you to throw away your life.

THE OLDEST SON: It hasn't started yet.

THE OLDER MOTHER: You're a good boy. You always were.

THE OLDEST SON: I'm going to become a chemical engineer and move back home.

THE OLDER MOTHER: You mustn't throw away your life.

THE OLDEST SON: I'm not throwing it away. They are.

(A DOOR OPENS. THE OLDEST SON STANDS UP. THE OLDER MOTHER LOOKS AT THE DOOR.)

■

(A FEW MEN ARE APPROACHING, CARRYING A BODY. THEY PASS BY "THE NEIGHBOR" AND "THE OTHER," WHO ARE STANDING IN THE CORRIDOR. "THE NEIGHBOR" AND "THE OTHER" MOVE TO THE SIDE.)

THE NEIGHBOR: I just finished.

THE OTHER: Again. Yes, that's usually how it is.

THE NEIGHBOR: Yes.

THE OTHER: That's what you usually say when you see me.

THE NEIGHBOR: Really.

THE OTHER: Why are you leaving now? This early.

THE NEIGHBOR: Well . . . I'm on leave for a couple of weeks.

THE OTHER: Really. Well, I guess . . . that's understandable.

THE NEIGHBOR: I can't put in the hours the way I should, anyway. I have to be with Anne Marie as long as . . . this last . . . the time she has left.

THE OTHER: Of course. You have enough to take care of her.

THE NEIGHBOR: We don't know how much time she has left. I'm no expert on that.

THE OTHER: Of course you have to be with her.

THE NEIGHBOR: I have to be there.

THE OTHER: Yes, you have to. (SHORT PAUSE) What?

THE NEIGHBOR: No, I . . . I got . . .

THE OTHER: Yes, you have to.

THE NEIGHBOR: Yes. Sure.

THE OTHER: How's she?

THE NEIGHBOR: Well, she's dying.

THE OTHER: Yes.

THE NEIGHBOR: Mostly she sleeps. They told me that she would at the end. Sometimes she's very clear. Clear and light, like before . . . as if she didn't have a body anymore. But now she looks thirty years older than what she'll ever be.

THE OTHER: Yes.

THE NEIGHBOR: The worst thing is . . . she doesn't want to die.

THE OTHER: No.

THE NEIGHBOR: She doesn't want to let go. (SILENCE) I have to think about Niklas, too. I don't want him to spend a lot of time with her

. . . only when she has the strength to see him. He's very good. Very calm and brave.

THE OTHER: Yes, children usually are at that age. How old is he?

THE NEIGHBOR: He'll be seven. In June. He's at his grandma's quite often. Yesterday he fell off his bike and broke his left arm. Now his arm is in a cast.

THE OTHER: That's too bad.

THE NEIGHBOR: It's just a small fracture, but still . . . (SILENCE) that's all I have to say.

THE OTHER: I know.

THE NEIGHBOR: What I need is to get myself into a drunken stupor and then fuck you to pieces.

THE OTHER: Anytime. My door is open. Whenever you want.

THE NEIGHBOR: Until I forget everything.

THE OTHER: Whenever you want.

THE NEIGHBOR: Yes, thank you.

THE OTHER: We could have a real orgy.

THE NEIGHBOR: Yes, my God.

THE OTHER: But don't wait too long.

■

THE MAN: Long time no see.

THE NEIGHBOR: Yes . . . maybe . . .

THE MAN: I used to live here.

THE NEIGHBOR: Aha.

THE MAN: A few of years ago. You did too.

THE NEIGHBOR: Yes, we . . .

THE MAN: And now I live here again.

THE NEIGHBOR: Yes.

THE MAN: Well, you have to put your hat somewhere. (SILENCE) Well, see you around.

THE NEIGHBOR: Sure.

THE MAN: Well, your wife . . .

THE NEIGHBOR: What about her?

THE MAN: Can't you take care of her?

THE NEIGHBOR: What? What are you talking about?

THE MAN: I said, can't you take care of her? (SILENCE) She asked me if I wanted a whore. I never saw her before. I just offered her a cigarette and then she asked if I wanted a whore. Well, not her anyway, the way she looks. Asked what I wanted to do. Said that we needed condoms. Asked if I knew of some quiet place. Said we could do it there. I'm an exhibitionist, she said. She said today is her daughter's birthday and she needed money to buy a gift for her.

■

THE MAN: Anyone home? (WALKS AROUND.) Where the hell are you? (OPENS THE DOOR TO THE BOY'S ROOM.) Are you sitting around again? (SHORT PAUSE) Why don't you answer when I call out for you? (SHORT PAUSE) Didn't you hear me, fucking kid? (SILENCE) What are you doing? (SILENCE) (WALKS INTO THE ROOM.) What's going on? (SILENCE) (GOES UP TO THE BOY.) Answer me when I'm talking to you. (SHORT PAUSE, GRABS HIS SHOULDER, TURNS HIM AROUND. THE BOY HAS PAINTED HIS

FACE COMPLETELY BLACK AND HIS HAIR IS HANGING OVER HIS FACE SO THAT WE CAN'T SEE IT.) What the hell is wrong with you? (THE BOY STANDS UP AND IS ABOUT TO LEAVE; THE MAN GRABS HIS WRIST.) Stay. I'm talking to you. Fucking ghost. Sit down.

THE BOY: Piss off.

THE MAN: Piss off? Are you crazy. (HITS THE BOY.) Sit, I said. (PULLS THE BOY DOWN; HOLDS HIM.) Listen to me. I'm your dad. Do you get it? Do you understand? I've made you with my own cock. That's something you can't get away from however much you try. Never. Ever. I am your goddamn dad, the only one you have, the only one you'll ever have, whatever you do. I'll be behind you in your tracks until you rot. And that's that.

THE BOY: Go to hell! Get out! Get back to the gutter where you belong! You're a piece of shit! I can't stand you. If you touch me I'll kill you!

THE MAN: Shut up. I'm the one responsible for you from here on. I'm going to take care of you and help you to become something in this fucking world. Now I'm the one making decisions here, do you understand? And from now on we'll be friends, father and son. Do you hear me? I don't want anything bad for you. If you treat me with respect I'll treat you with respect. If not, I'll keep hurting you. That's how simple it is. Your choice. Just as well that you stop your shit right away, because it'll be the way I'm telling you, whether you want it or not. Do you understand? You can choose the easy way or the hard way. It is what it is. (THE BOY TURNS HIS FACE AWAY. THE MAN GRABS IT AND TURNS THE BOY'S FACE TOWARD HIM.) You need me. You need me much more than I need you. You need someone to teach you what life is about. (THE BOY CLOSES HIS EYES.) Look at me. (HITS HIM.) Hell, if I tell you to look at me, you look at me. (THE BOY KEEPS HIS EYES SHUT.) My own dad died a couple of days ago. My old man died. Sick and old. No one cared about him. But I was there when he died. I held his hand, the son of a bitch. I hadn't seen him for seven years. He was a tough, old man, a devil, but it was good that I could say goodbye to him before he passed away. He drank everything to pieces. I hated him, I did, don't think anything else. But he left. And that was the best thing he could've done. I haven't been God's best child myself, but I'm back here to set things right and to take care of my family. Don't you understand that? I could've been away right now, but I'm not. I'm here. I'm not like my dad. I take responsibility. I behave. I do what's right. I work, and I get my salary. That's all you can do. I want you to understand that. I'm going to take care of your mother and you and your sick sister. I'm going to put everything right again. Do you understand? (SILENCE) Answer me. (SHORT PAUSE) What the hell, look at me and give me an answer. (SILENCE) (EXHAUSTED) Say something. (SILENCE) She's having a baby. Your mom. She's having a baby. (SILENCE) Say something . . . talk to me.

THE MOM: (ENTERS.) Is this where you are? (SILENCE) What are you doing? (THE BOY STANDS UP AND GOES TO HER.) Rainer.

THE BOY: (HITS HER IN HER STOMACH WITH ALL HIS MIGHT.) Fucking whore! You're a rotten fucking whore.

■

(DURING THE WHOLE SCENE THE SISTER IS KEEPING HER EYES SHUT.)

THE BOY: Aren't you going to eat that one?

THE SISTER: No, too much sugar. (SHORT PAUSE) You can have it.

THE BOY TAKES THE ITALIAN COOKIE AND EATS IT.) I have a whole bag full. (SHORT PAUSE) Andrej brings them to me. But I don't really like them. He wants to marry me he says.

THE BOY: Who's he?

THE SISTER: Andrej. He works nights here. (SHORT PAUSE) I'm afraid of him.

THE BOY: Why?

THE SISTER: He's sicker than the ones in here. I think that's why he's here. He lives with his mom. He likes girls who like them to be hard.

THE BOY: Hard?

THE SISTER: Towards them. (SILENCE) Great that you came to see me.

THE BOY: Yes.

THE SISTER: But you don't have to . . .

THE BOY: How long will you be here?

THE SISTER: Yes, that's the question.

THE BOY: Are you feeling any better?

THE SISTER: Today I do. (SILENCE) The other day we went out, everyone at the same time, like kindergarten kids, all in a row, except for one who had jumped out the window and is sitting in a wheelchair. The weather was nice. We went down to the beach. (IS WRITING SOMETHING DOWN.) She's in a wheelchair. Her dad strangled a woman while she was watching. She saw how he did it. She had said she wanted to leave him and he got angry. And then he strangled her. She was sitting there holding their little baby in her lap. Then she called the police. That's the only thing she talks about. Her dad. (CONTINUES TO WRITE SOMETHING DOWN.)

THE BOY: What are you writing?

THE SISTER: He bought this one for me when I said I needed one.

THE BOY: What are you writing?

THE SISTER: What she said . . . what the police said when she called.

THE BOY: What did they say?

THE SISTER: That's what I'm trying to remember. I write down things I need to remember.

THE BOY: Is he in jail?

THE SISTER: That I have to write down.

THE BOY: How long will he be in jail?

THE SISTER: Maybe it's better not to remember.

THE BOY: What?

THE SISTER: What I'm writing, so I don't forget.

THE BOY: Which prison is the closest to where we live?

THE SISTER: It's strange. (SILENCE) Could two different things happen on the same day in different places at the same time? Can you be part of two different things on the same day at the same time?

THE BOY: Same time? How?

THE SISTER: Well. I was walking with the others and then we went to a café down by the beach and I had a sugar-free coconut cookie, but at the same time, the same day I was at home and he came out of the bathroom and said that he wasn't going to use a condom, that he would do it in the ass. How could that happen?
THE BOY: I don't know.

THE SISTER: Me neither . . . but I've written it down. It was the same day. It says so here. Saturday, April 14. He said that now I'm big enough so it'll work. It won't hurt anymore. But it does hurt. It always hurts.

(SILENCE)

THE BOY: When will you be allowed to come home?

THE SISTER: Home?

THE BOY: Yes.

THE SISTER: I guess that's here?

THE BOY: What?

THE SISTER: Home.

THE BOY: Didn't they tell you anything?

THE SISTER: No.

THE BOY: Don't do it. Don't come home.

THE SISTER: No.

THE BOY: He's back. (SILENCE) Bert. (SILENCE) He's living there again.

THE SISTER: I have to go somewhere where it's really hot. Where it's burning hot all the time.

THE BOY: They're having a baby. He knocked her up again.

(SILENCE)

THE SISTER: Are you leaving now?

THE BOY: No.

THE SISTER: When?

THE BOY: I don't know where to go. I've no place to go. I don't want to go there. Go home.

THE SISTER: It was nice that you came.

THE BOY: Can't we go someplace where I can smoke? I'm smoking now.

THE SISTER: I don't like reading the ending of a book. I don't want to read the last three chapters. I don't want to know what happens. It's been long since I read a book. Andrej gave me this one, but I don't want to read it. Every day he asks me if I like it. Why I'm not reading it. It was very expensive.

THE BOY: How could you read when you never open your eyes . . . when you can't see?

THE SISTER: No. You're so silly.

THE BOY: I am?

(SILENCE)

THE SISTER: There's an angel standing behind me. His arm is around my neck. Do you see him?

THE BOY: No.

THE SISTER: Don't you see him?

■

("THE BOY" IS LIGHTING A CIGARETTE OUTSIDE, IN THE BACK OF THE HOSPITAL. HENRY IS PASSING BY, DEATHLY TIRED, HIS FACE IS GREY.) (SILENCE) HENRY SITS NEXT TO A BED WHERE AN OLD, PALE MAN IS LYING ABSOLUTELY STILL.) (SILENCE)

HENRY: Are you awake?

(SILENCE)

THE ELDER: Help.

HENRY: Help?

THE ELDER: (IN A WEAK VOICE) Help . . .

HENRY: With what? (SILENCE) Have you been eating? (SHORT PAUSE) Did you eat? Are you eating? (SHORT PAUSE) You have to eat. Soon there's nothing left of you.

THE ELDER: Help me. Who are you?

HENRY: (BENDS DOWN AND TAKES THE HAND OF THE ELDER) It's me . . . Henry.

THE ELDER: Help me. (TRIES TO SIT UP.)

HENRY: Yes, take it easy. (SILENCE) I just drove someone here.

THE ELDER: Him. (THE ONLY THING MOVING ARE HIS EYES, DARTING BACK AND FORTH, FRIGHTENED.)

HENRY: I had a fare over here. To the birthing clinic. (SHORT PAUSE) I forgot to turn on the meter. I didn't even notice until I stopped by the entrance As if I didn't already have losses all over the place.

THE ELDER: He came back. Last night.

HENRY: Who?

THE ELDER: The same one.

HENRY: Aha.

THE ELDER: Help me.

HENRY: Yes . . . with what? (SILENCE) You know I'm going back in a couple of weeks for Jasenko's wedding. Before she gives birth. In September, he says. It's better they're married before. I guess the whole village will be at the party, the ones who are left anyway. Not too many I think. I guess I'll stay for a couple of months. See if I can do something about the house. (THE ELDER IS CRYING.) Did you hear me? (SHORT PAUSE) You're going to be a Great Grandpa. (SHORT PAUSE) I'll do a video so that you can look later. (SILENCE) What's wrong?

THE ELDER: It's hell.

HENRY: Yes, that's true. It is hell. But what can we do?

THE ELDER: He was here. (SILENCE) Him. (HE MOVES HIS HANDS IN THE AIR LIKE A NEWBORN BABY.) He was here last night.

HENRY: Last night?

THE ELDER: Yes, last night. This past night.

HENRY: I've talked to them. He isn't supposed to work here anymore. Not on this floor. They promised.

THE ELDER: When I was asleep.

HENRY: I've told them.

THE ELDER: He was in my bed. He hugged me.

HENRY: How the hell is it possible he's still here?

THE ELDER: He was laying behind me. The same one. He told me to be quiet.

HENRY: Last night?

THE ELDER: My ass hurts.

HENRY: I'm going to the police. I told them I'd go to the police if it happened one more time.

THE ELDER: I scream and I scream but no one hears me. No one hears me. (PAUSE) They don't come.

■

(HENRY BUMPS INTO "THE MOM" IN THE STREET.)

THE MOM: Are you off already?

HENRY: No, is that what it looks like?

THE MOM: No, it's . . .

HENRY: When the hell am I ever off?

THE MOM: No, no . . . not if you have a job to go to.

HENRY: Yes, why the hell do I do it? Why the hell am I so fucking stupid that I try to do the right thing? Because that's how I was brought up, not to depend on others. I guess soon they'll even steal those fucking walkers and sell them.

THE MOM: Yes, isn't it terrible . . . the way everything has changed?

HENRY: Yes, a fucking gangster society.

THE MOM: But what can you do?

HENRY: Soon I've had enough, if not already. I can hardly stand being in the car. My back is shot, and I have no feeling in my hands, not in the right one anyway. The other night some fucking idiot threw up all over my back seat, and I made him pay for it, since I couldn't take any more fares that night. I had to drive somewhere to get it cleaned up. Three times they tried but it still stinks.

THE MOM: Yes, it's . . . I have to . . .

HENRY: Everything is shit . . . up to one's neck in shit . . . other people's shit.

THE MOM: I have to go.

HENRY: Yes, go.

THE MOM: Yes.

∎

THE MOM: Are you here? (SILENCE) Why aren't you dressed? (SILENCE) It's starting in an hour. We have to leave right now to make it.
THE BOY: I'm not going.

THE MOM: Did you wash up?

THE BOY: You go. I'm not going.

THE MOM: You aren't going?

THE BOY: No.

THE MOM: Now put on your suit and tie and clean underwear. (SILENCE) Everything is on your bed.

THE BOY: I'm not going.

THE MOM: What's wrong with you?

THE BOY: I don't feel good, my stomach hurts.

THE MOM: Everybody will be there. The whole school is going there . . . to the church.

THE BOY: Not me.

THE MOM: Of course you are.

THE BOY: No.

THE MOM: I bought you a new suit and everything, and a new shirt.

THE BOY: Don't you hear what I'm saying?

THE MOM: I'm sure it'll be a very nice ceremony . . . with all the kids there singing. (SHORT PAUSE) Rainer?

THE BOY: What the hell, stop nagging.

THE MOM: Hurry up, get dressed. (SILENCE) What will I tell them about you not being there?

THE BOY: You don't have to say a fucking thing. You never say anything anyway.
THE MOM: What am I supposed to tell them . . . tell her mother?

THE BOY: You just stand there not saying a fucking word.

(SILENCE)

THE MOM: Rainer . . .

THE BOY: You never say anything. You don't exist. You make me feel ashamed.

THE MOM: I see.

THE BOY: Because you're so out of it—just a fucking empty space.

THE MOM: Well, I'm sorry . . . but you're still going, aren't you . . . she went to school with you . . . you knew her.

THE BOY: I don't know anyone. Not a fucking sole. Hope you know that.

THE MOM: What's gotten into you? Why do you talk like this? (TRIES TO TOUCH HIM.) Why don't you . . .

THE BOY: (HITS HER.) Don't touch me, you fucking whore.

THE MOM: What's wrong?

THE BOY: Don't even try touching me, you fucking cunt. (HITS HER, KICKS HER, PUSHES HER DOWN ON THE FLOOR, CONTINUES TO HIT HER.) You are going to have a kid with that fucking asshole, even though you know what he did.

THE MOM: I don't know anything.

THE BOY: You know. You knew. The whole time you knew.

THE MOM: I didn't know anything.

THE BOY: You knew. You knew what he was doing.

THE MOM: No.

THE BOY: You knew.

■

THE MOM: Are you home already?

THE MAN: Yes, as you can see.

THE MOM: Yes, was it difficult . . .

THE MAN: What?

THE MOM: Well . . . the traffic?

THE MAN: There wasn't any fucking traffic. Just straight away home.

THE MOM: Well, that's good anyway.

THE MAN: There's no real traffic here . . . to speak of.

THE MOM: Since it's Friday. . . . Aren't you coming in?

THE MAN: She's inside. Don't you see her standing here? (SILENCE) So, how was the funeral?

THE MOM: We didn't go.

THE MAN: You didn't go? Why?

THE MOM: His stomach was hurting.

THE MAN: Stomach?

THE MOM: I guess he had a stomachache. So, we stayed home.

THE MAN: What the hell, we'd even bought him a new suit and shirt and tie, so that he would be there.

THE MOM: He'll have to use them some other time . . . for his graduation maybe.

THE MAN: We spent a lot of money.

THE MOM: It's not wasted anyway.

THE MAN: Where's he? Is he in there?

THE MOM: No, he went out.

THE MAN: He went out? When?

THE MOM: I don't know . . . I was down in the laundry room. He was gone when I came back.

THE MAN: Then he might as well stay out. Why the hell am I spending money on him?

THE MOM: I don't know what it is. That's . . . (SILENCE) Aren't you going to take your coat off?

THE SISTER: No.

THE MOM: Yes . . .

THE SISTER: I'm not staying.

THE MAN: You're here until Sunday.

THE SISTER: Why?

THE MOM: I think that was the plan.

(SILENCE)

THE MAN: Yes, take your coat off. ("THE SISTER" VERY SLOWLY TAKES OFF HER COAT. ALL HER MOVEMENTS ARE EXTREMELY SLOW.) Yes, there's no hurry.

THE SISTER: How long am I here for?

THE MAN: We told you, until Sunday.

THE SISTER: Am I going home then?

THE MAN: Home?

THE SISTER: Yes.

THE MAN: This is your home. The only home you have. (SILENCE) You look all grown up.

THE MOM: She's nineteen.

THE MAN: I know.

THE MOM: Already.

THE MAN: Yes, time flies. More or less. Let's go in and sit down.

THE MOM: Yes, let's . . .

THE MAN: What's with your face?

THE MOM: My face?

THE MAN: Yes, what the hell is going on with your face?

THE MOM: Nothing. I . . .

THE MAN: Did you take a beating?

THE MOM: No, it's . . . no, I fell. . . . I slipped down there in the laundry room . . . I slipped and hit . . . I hit the table . . . it hurt like hell.

THE MAN: Bullshit. That's just bullshit. He did it. That fucking kid. He hit you.

THE MOM: No, I slipped. It's true. I wasn't careful.

THE MAN: Hell no, don't try anything with me. I can see that you didn't slip. He hit you.

THE MOM: I slipped. I'm a real klutz. It's true

THE MAN: How the hell do you slip falling forwards on your face? You'd have fallen backwards.

THE MOM: But I did. I fell forwards.

THE MAN: Well, you can try.

THE MOM: I'm not trying.

THE MAN: You're trying to protect him, but that's over now. This is the end of his stupidities. And this is the end of you always standing up for him. If he doesn't learn now, he never will. Everything could go to hell.

THE SISTER: I guess only you can.

THE MAN: What did you say?

THE MOM: No, be quiet.

THE SISTER: Hit someone.

THE MAN: What are you saying?

THE SISTER: That it's only you who's allowed to hit someone.

THE MAN: I haven't hit anyone. Who did I hit?

THE MOM: No one. Nothing.

THE MAN: Well, I hope not.

THE MOM: It's true. I slipped and hit the table down there. The lighting is terrible. You can't see where you're going.

THE MAN: He's absolutely crazy. You can't even talk to him.

(SILENCE)

THE MOM: How about some food? . . . What do you think?

THE MAN: What does that have to do with this?

THE MOM: No, but . . . (SILENCE) Sanna, do you want to see if there's anything on television?

THE MAN: It's Friday. Nothing but crap. Only idiots spend their lives in front of the TV.

THE SISTER: I want to go to bed.

THE MOM: Already?

THE SISTER: I'm tired.

THE MAN: But you just got here.

THE SISTER: I'm tired.

THE MOM: You are? Is it the medication?

THE SISTER: I'm tired.

THE MAN: Who the hell isn't tired?

THE MOM: We want to know how you're doing.

THE SISTER: Fine.

THE MAN: Fine?

THE SISTER: Yes.

THE MAN: What do mean by "fine"?

THE SISTER: It's fine.

THE MAN: In what way is it fine?

THE SISTER: Well, OK. (SHORT PAUSE) Can I lock the door?

THE MAN: What door?

THE SISTER: Is it possible to lock . . . the door?

THE MAN: Why would you do that?

THE SISTER: To the room?

THE MAN: Here we don't lock anything. This is a home.

THE SISTER: I have to lock the door.

THE MAN: There are so many things you HAVE to do, don't you?

THE SISTER: I want to have it locked. I want to lock the door.

THE MOM: Now they're gone.

THE MAN: What did you say?

THE MOM: Now they're gone.

THE MAN: What?

THE MOM: The tulips.

THE MAN: Yea, the tulips.

THE MOM: I threw them out. They were dead.

THE MAN: That's what happens. (SILENCE) Where's the laundry? (SHORT PAUSE) That you washed? (SILENCE) Where is the laundry, the clean laundry? (SHORT PAUSE) Did you put it away already?

■

THE MAN: It's just me.

THE SISTER: What do you want?

THE MAN: Are you awake?

THE SISTER: What do you want?

THE MAN: Why aren't you in bed already?

THE SISTER: (TURNS ON A LAMP.)

THE MAN: Are you just sitting here?

THE SISTER: What do you want?

(SILENCE)

THE MAN: May I sit . . . here? (SITS NEXT TO HER ON THE BED. THE SISTER IS ABOUT TO GET UP.) No, stay.

THE SISTER: What do you want?

THE MAN: What I want . . .nothing, really. Just wanted to talk. I'm trying . . . (SILENCE) Why . . . it is like this. I'd like to know why. What did I do wrong? Well, all kinds of things I guess. Why are you sick . . . I'd really like to understand? Why?

THE SISTER: I'm not sick.

THE MAN: You aren't?

THE SISTER: I'm not sick.

THE MAN: No. So, what are you then?

THE SISTER: I'm not sick.

THE MAN: Why aren't you getting any better then?

THE SISTER: You can't heal something that isn't an illness.

THE MAN: Really . . . well, I don't know. (SILENCE) Well, then I don't know what it is. But I want to help you. That's all I want. I'm trying the best I can. It's not easy for me either. Did you know that your grandfather died? (SILENCE). He died last Monday. I was there. I was with him. (SHORT PAUSE) You met him, didn't you? We went to see him when you were a little girl. I guess you were around four years old. Do you remember that? (SILENCE). Don't you remember that? In his house. His apartment. He lived in an apartment building, but he had his own spot for growing things down in the yard. He grew vegetables and flowers. . . . He had a real garden going. He came from farm country. I guess his dad had been some kind of farmer. I never knew him. He died long before I was born. You know, he had a real vegetable garden among the apartment houses. He never felt at home . . . except when he was gardening, planting stuff and weeding. (SHORT PAUSE) But it's as if you and I don't know each other. I guess it's my fault. I'm sure I wasn't the world's best. . . . I was young and difficult, and we had no money when you were little. You had to choose between a hot dog and an ice-cream cone. We couldn't afford both. (SILENCE) But you, my family, is all I fucking have. (SHORT PAUSE) I don't want it to go to hell . . . again. It can't be just my fault . . . that it worked out like this. . . . I mean, it isn't fucking normal that he can't go to the funeral for one of his classmates. That's what you do. However much fucking pain you have in your stomach. (SILENCE) (HE TAKES HER HAND.)

THE SISTER: No.

THE MAN: Sanna.

THE SISTER: Don't touch me.

THE MAN: What? I just wanted to . . .

THE SISTER: Don't ever touch me again.

THE MAN: What's wrong?

THE SISTER: You can't do that ever again.

THE MAN: Do what?

THE SISTER: No. No. No. No.

THE MAN: What the hell, stop it! What the hell is going on? Stop screaming!

("THE MOM" COMES IN.)

THE SISTER: No. No. No.

THE MOM: What are you doing in here?

THE MAN: (TRIES TO STAND UP.) I'm trying to talk to her.

THE MOM: Leave her alone. You may never touch her again!

THE MAN: I'm trying to talk to her.

("THE MOM" PICKS UP THE LAMP AND HITS HIM ON THE HEAD. SHE KEEPS HITTING HIM. SINCE SHE PULLS THE CORD OUT OF THE WALL SOCKET, THE LIGHT GOES OUT AND THE STAGE GOES DARK.)

■

HENRY: Aha? (SILENCE) Where are you going? (SHORT PAUSE) Where do you want to go?

THE SISTER: Yes, I want to.

HENRY: What? (SILENCE) Where am I supposed to drive you?

THE SISTER: I don't know.

HENRY: You don't know?

THE SISTER: Home.

HENRY: Home.

THE SISTER: Yes. Home.

HENRY: Aha. So where's that?

THE SISTER: Home.

(SILENCE)

HENRY: I have to know where to drive you.

THE SISTER: Away.

HENRY: Away?

THE SISTER: Yes. Home. (SILENCE) Can't you drive me there?

HENRY: Hell, I can drive you anywhere, just as long as I know where that is.

THE SISTER: Home would be good.

HENRY: Aren't you feeling well?

THE SISTER: No.

HENRY: No, I can see that.

THE SISTER: I've never felt good.

HENRY: Really, no, no it's . . .

THE SISTER: I've been pretending.

HENRY: No, who feels good here . . . in this country?

THE SISTER: I've been pretending . . . feeling good.

HENRY: Yes, yes . . .

THE SISTER: So that Mom wouldn't be sad.

HENRY: Yea, that's . . . (SILENCE) but really, I can't just sit here.

THE SISTER: No.

HENRY: But you aren't wearing any shoes.

THE SISTER: No. Look.

HENRY: Where are they?

THE SISTER: Where they are?

HENRY: Yes?

THE SISTER: I don't know.

HENRY: (NOTICES THAT SHE IS LOOKING AROUND WITH FEAR IN HER EYES.) There's no other solution but for you to get out of my cab.

THE SISTER: Yes.

HENRY: I can't sit here all night, however nice it might be, and lose money. Can't do that.

THE SISTER: I want to go home.

HENRY: Yes, I would like to drive you home, but I don't know how, since I don't know where it is, and you don't either. I could drive into town if you could pay for it, but then you've got to show me the money.

(SILENCE)

THE SISTER: No.

HENRY: So you can't pay me?

THE SISTER: I've no money.

HENRY: No.

THE SISTER: I think they are in the social security office.

(SILENCE)

HENRY: Where were you . . . before you got into my cab?

THE SISTER: I . . . I think I was in . . . in hell.

HENRY: In hell?

THE SISTER: I think that's what it's called.

HENRY: Oh. There.

THE SISTER: Yes, that's where I am.

HENRY: Yes, it's everywhere, isn't it?

THE SISTER: No, I'm in mine.

HENRY: And I'm in mine.

THE SISTER: Maybe it's hard to find.

HENRY: Maybe it's the same.

THE SISTER: Why?

HENRY: Same hell.

THE SISTER: No . . . I've never seen you before.

HENRY: No, but . . . it's big.

THE SISTER: Yes. (SHORT PAUSE) It's really big.

HENRY Yes, there are too many there. Many too many. (SILENCE) What's your name?

THE SISTER: Virginia.

HENRY: Virginia?

THE SISTER: Yes. Virgin.

HENRY: Well, my name is Henry. (SILENCE) But my real name is Jasenko. I changed it to Henry when I started to drive a cab. But what the hell am I doing with that name? Henry. What kind of fucking name is that? I'm taking back my real name again. (SHORT PAUSE) I've turned off my phone. I can't stand listening to them. Right now there are only bar "pickups." Since it's Friday and the weather is fucking horrible, the twentieth of April, and the snow is coming down like crazy and not a fucking soul is outside. (SHORT PAUSE) What am I to do with you? I don't know. (SHORT PAUSE) I was trying to get a couple of more fares and then put the car away and go home and sleep. (SHORT PAUSE) I can't sleep anymore. Never a whole night. No sleep at all. In bed staring at the ceiling, twisting and turning. I don't understand what I'm doing here. In this country. It's not my country, however good it is here. Nothing wrong with it, I'm sure, a fucking good country for the people who live here, who call this home. But I don't feel at home here. I try not to think about it; I try to fit in, adjust to the fact that it is what it is. This is what has happened to me, but it's getting harder and harder . . . everything. I guess it doesn't have anything to do with this country really. I haven't had any real problems. . . . I mean, not worse than other people; but now my dad is in a nursing home and he doesn't want anything but to die, he doesn't want to live another day. He says that a man has to know what he's dying for, and when . . . and he says that for him the time is now . . . now that they have him wearing some fucking diapers. He who always did everything for himself. There's nothing left, and everyone he knew is still back home or dead already. Only the house is left, and he'll never see it again. He's too old and sick to travel, and what the fuck would he do there? . . . But, still, that's where he wants to go to live out his final days. . . . I'm trying to get him moved from where he is now, because there've been some problems with one of the staff members, someone who's still working there; but I can't get him in anywhere else . . . since we don't have the money for some private care. I don't know what's happening to him right now, if he's crying out for help and no one is showing up to help him. Anything can happen. They run around in the corridors all night long and try to open doors to . . . well, I don't know where they think they're going. Sometimes he's sitting in his own shit all day long, and he cries like a child when I visit him. It's not human. (STARTS UP THE CAR.)

THE SISTER: On "American Idol" they cry all the time.

HENRY: Who?

THE SISTER: They cry when they talk about some relative who's died, some Grandma or Uncle. Then they cry.

HENRY: I guess they want the people to vote for them.

THE SISTER: And then the people in the Day Room cry too.

∎

HENRY: (WALKS THROUGH THE SLIDING DOORS. HE IS CARRYING HIS FATHER, WHO LOOKS LIKE A CHILD IN HIS ARMS, WRAPPED IN A HOSPITAL BLANKET.) Everything is fine. Now it's fine. It'll be fine. Nothing bad will happen to you anymore.

THE ELDER: Where am I?

HENRY: We're going home. Not a fucking soul will touch you again.

THE ELDER: It hurts.

HENRY: Yes, but not ever again. Everything is fine. We're going home.

THE ELDER: Yes.

HENRY: Going home.

THE ELDER: I don't have a suitcase.

HENRY: No, you don't need a suitcase.

THE ELDER: I have nothing.

HENRY: No, I know. Now everything is fine. (TO THE SISTER) Please open the door. (SHORT PAUSE) Open the door. (SHE OPENS IT.) He has to sit there, where you're sitting. You have to leave now.

THE SISTER: Where am I supposed to go?

HENRY I don't know. But you have to get out of the car. I'm driving my dad home. He has to go home. He can't stay there any longer. You have to get out. (THE SISTER GETS OUT OF THE CAR.) There's a hospital over there. Just straight ahead to the right. On the other side of the building. That's where the reception is. They'll help you. They should help you. (PUTS HIS DAD IN THE BACKSEAT, FASTENS THE SAFETY BELT.) Let's drive home.

■

(THE SISTER IS SITTING ON A PLASTIC CHAIR IN A BIG WAITING ROOM. ACROSS FROM HER IS THE DEAD GIRL'S MOTHER.)

THE MOTHER OF THE GIRL: Don't say anything.

HER FRIEND: (SITTING NEXT TO HER, HOLDING HER HAND.) No.

THE MOTHER OF THE GIRL: Whatever you do.

HER FRIEND: No.

THE MOTHER OF THE GIRL: I can't stand any more words.

HER FRIEND: I know.

THE MOTHER OF THE GIRL: I don't want to listen to any more words.

HER FRIEND: No, I won't . . . you know that.

THE MOTHER OF THE GIRL: They don't help.

HER FRIEND: No. (SQUEEZES HER HAND.) They don't help. There, there. (SILENCE) I know . . . I know how it was when Nils passed away.

THE MOTHER OF THE GIRL: You don't know. No one knows.

HER FRIEND: I mean . . .

MOTHER OF THE GIRL: No.

(SILENCE)

HER FRIEND: Did Sven say when he was coming?

THE MOTHER OF THE GIRL: I don't give a damn if he comes.

HER FRIEND: No.

THE MOTHER OF THE GIRL: He hasn't bothered with her before, so why should he show up now?

HER FRIEND: No.

THE MOTHER OF THE GIRL: I hope he'll see her lying there, so that he'll understand what he has missed.

HER FRIEND: Yes, it's . . .

THE MOTHER OF THE GIRL: That fucking swine. Why doesn't he take his fucking life and shove it up his ass. (SILENCE) Don't even talk about him. I can't stand hearing his name. He didn't even send her a birthday card . . . or bother to pick up a telephone. But she had stopped waiting for . . . she had no hope left . . . she had realized what a fucking, worthless shit he is. He doesn't even exist.

HER FRIEND: No, of course, the way he's been.

THE MOTHER OF THE GIRL: He hasn't been at all. (SILENCE) Good God . . . how can I go home?

HER FRIEND: You can come . . .

THE MOTHER OF THE GIRL: What's there to go home to?

HER FRIEND: You're welcome to come home with me.

THE MOTHER OF THE GIRL: All her stuff . . . all her clothes . . . her stuffed animals . . .

HER FRIEND: Wouldn't it be better if you stayed with me for a couple of days?

THE MOTHER OF THE GIRL: Nothing would be better.

HER FRIEND: No. (SILENCE) I wish there was something I could do.

THE MOTHER OF THE GIRL: What?

HER FRIEND: I don't know.

THE MOTHER OF THE GIRL: No. (SILENCE) I don't know what you could do.

HER FRIEND: I thought since you called me . . .

(SILENCE)

THE MOTHER OF THE GIRL: You could hug me.

HER FRIEND: Yes.

THE MOTHER OF THE GIRL: Why don't you?

HER FRIEND: Sorry, I'm sorry.

THE MOTHER OF THE GIRL: Well, hug me then.

HER FRIEND: (HUGS HER)

THE MOTHER OF THE GIRL: Harder.

HER FRIEND: Sure, Sure.

THE MOTHER OF THE GIRL: Come on.

HER FRIEND: What?

THE MOTHER OF THE GIRL: Come on.

HER FRIEND: Come on?

THE MOTHER OF THE GIRL: Yes, come on, I said. (SHE BEGINS TO CARESS HIM, HIS FACE, HIS NECK, STARTS TO UNBUTTON HIS SHIRT, THEN SHE TRIES TO UNDO HIS PANTS.)

HER FRIEND: No, no, not here. Wait. Wait . . .

THE MOTHER OF THE GIRL: What kind of fucking buttons are these? It's like they were nailed shut. (CARESSES HIS CHEST.) You better unbutton these yourself. (FEELS SOMETHING WITH HER FINGERS.) What's this?

HER FRIEND: It's just a tattoo.

THE MOTHER OF THE GIRL: It is? (LOOKS AT IT.) What does it say?

HER FRIEND: Don't you see what it says?

THE MOTHER OF THE GIRL: No, what does it say?

HER FRIEND: "My God, my God, why have you forsaken me?"

THE MOTHER OF THE GIRL: Is that what it says?

HER FRIEND: Yes, that's what Christ says hanging on the cross . . . before he dies.

THE MOTHER OF THE GIRL: Are you religious?

HER FRIEND: Yes.

THE MOTHER OF THE GIRL: (STOPS CARESSING HIM.) I'm not. How could I be?

HER FRIEND: I know that there's a God.

THE MOTHER OF THE GIRL: Who's allowed this to happen?

HER FRIEND: It's not God's fault. God didn't do it.

THE MOTHER OF THE GIRL: There's no God . . . who takes my little girl from me.

HER FRIEND: Once I didn't think so either, until I met him. (SILENCE) You can't understand it until you meet him. Then you understand everything.

THE MOTHER OF THE GIRL: Look, she's looking at us.

HER FRIEND: Who?

THE MOTHER OF THE GIRL: The girl . . . who's sitting over there.

HER FRIEND: Let her look.

THE MOTHER OF THE GIRL: What's wrong with her?

HER FRIEND: If you can't show sorrow here . . . then, where could you show it?

■

THE IRANIAN: (PASSES BY.) Are you still here? (SHORT PAUSE) They didn't help you yet?

THE SISTER: No.

THE IRANIAN: They didn't?

THE SISTER: No.

THE IRANIAN: They'll soon be here.

(SILENCE)

THE SISTER: Do you have a cigarette?

THE IRANIAN: No, I don't smoke. I stopped eighteen years ago. (SHORT PAUSE) Everything will be all right.

THE SISTER: Yea, I guess.

THE IRANIAN: (GOES INTO AN OFFICE, SITS DOWN BY A DESK AND TURNS ON THE COMPUTER. AFTER A WHILE, ON THE SCREEN THERE IS A PICTURE OF A WHITE ROOM FAR AWAY WITH AN OLD WOMAN WAITING.) Mom? (SILENCE) Mom, do you see me?

THE OLD IRANIAN: Says something that can't be heard.

THE IRANIAN: You have to turn up the sound. (SHORT PAUSE) I can't hear you. Turn up the sound. (SHORT PAUSE) Do you hear me?

THE OLD IRANIAN: Says something in her native tongue.

THE IRANIAN: Now I hear you.

THE OLD IRANIAN: Where are you?

THE IRANIAN: How are you?

THE OLD IRANIAN: Are you coming home? (PAUSE) When are you coming home?

THE IRANIAN: One of these days. I don't know when. (SHORT PAUSE) You look tired. Are you feeling OK?

THE OLD IRANIAN: I pray to God . . . every day.

THE IRANIAN: Are you taking your medicine?

THE OLD IRANIAN: Yes, I'm taking my medicine.

THE IRANIAN: You have to.

THE OLD IRANIAN: Where are you?

THE IRANIAN: I'm working. I'm in my office. In the hospital, where I work. I'll be working all night.

THE OLD IRANIAN: There are many sick people here. Many, many sick people.

THE IRANIAN: I know. I know there are many.

THE OLD IRANIAN: But no one helping them.

THE IRANIAN: No, I know. (SHORT PAUSE) Sit a little closer. I can't see you. You're disappearing on me. You've got to sit still. I want to see your face.

THE OLD IRANIAN: I thought I heard someone at the door. (SILENCE) Was there someone? I pray every day. I pray to God that you'll be back here with me before it's too late.

THE IRANIAN: Yes.

THE OLD IRANIAN: You're the only one I've left. Soon it'll be too late.

THE IRANIAN: Well . . . we don't know what will happen. One day we'll see each other again.

(SILENCE)

THE OLD IRANIAN: Yes, we'll pray to God . . .

THE IRANIAN: You have to take your medicine every morning and night. Promise me that.

THE OLD IRANIAN: What's the use?

THE IRANIAN: Promise me. (SILENCE) Mom, I've got to go. (SHORT PAUSE) I love you. I miss you.

THE OLD IRANIAN: Aha.

THE IRANIAN: You know I do. I'll call you tomorrow. (SILENCE) Are you still there?

THE OLD IRANIAN: Yes, I'm here.

(SILENCE)

∎

(THE IRANIAN WALKS OUT OF HER OFFICE. THE SISTER IS STILL SITTING IN THE SAME WAY AS BEFORE. THE DOCTOR, WHOSE WIFE WAS EXPECTING A BABY, WALKS TOWARD THE IRANIAN.)

THE IRANIAN: Are you on call tonight? I thought you were off.

THE DOCTOR: I have a daughter! She's wonderful. Five pounds, six ounces. Twenty-one inches. She's amazing. Beautiful. Divine.

THE IRANIAN: Great.

THE DOCTOR: It only took an hour. She was out in just one hour. I cut the naval cord myself. Just one hour from the time we arrived to the time she was sucking on the breast. It was so wonderful. Anna was so beautiful. The most beautiful thing I've ever seen. I'm staying here tonight. I brought her coffee and a cheese sandwich. I'm just going downstairs for a smoke.

THE IRANIAN: Yes, why don't you.

THE DOCTOR: She's so beautiful. So tiny. A tiny, wrinkled bottom.

THE IRANIAN: Yes.

THE DOCTOR: When she came out . . . (SILENCE)

THE IRANIAN: Please wish her well from me.

THE DOCTOR: How old are yours?

THE IRANIAN: I don't have any . . . she would have been fourteen by now.

THE DOCTOR: I see. Well, I'm so sorry.

■

THE IRANIAN (WHO IS PREGNANT—WHICH WE DIDN'T NOTICE UNTIL NOW—IS WALKING TOWARD US HOLDING THE HAND OF A SMALL CHILD. THE CHILD IS CARRYING A STUFFED ANIMAL.) Are you going to show your drawing to Daddy?

THE LITTLE ONE: No.

THE IRANIAN: Of course you are.

THE LITTLE ONE: I don't want to.

THE IRANIAN: It's the first time you ever drew a person, with eyes and everything. He'll be so happy when he looks at it.

THE LITTLE ONE: Her name is Olle.

THE IRANIAN: Olle?

THE LITTLE ONE: Olle.

THE IRANIAN: His name. He's a boy. If it's a boy you say "his name." If it's a girl you say "her name."

THE LITTLE ONE: Yes, that's her name. I want to open the door. (SHE OPENS THE DOOR. THEY ENTER AN APARTMENT WHERE EVERYTHING IN IT SEEMS TO BE BROKEN. THE BROTHER IS SITTING BY HIS COMPUTER.)

THE IRANIAN: What happened?

THE BROTHER: What does it look like? (SILENCE) I came home and this is what it looked like.

THE IRANIAN: Where's she? Where's Seluah?

THE BROTHER: Gone.

THE IRANIAN: Gone?

THE BROTHER: She's been gone for three years.

THE IRANIAN: She isn't home?

THE BROTHER: In the bedroom. Sleeping. She got tired after breaking everything.

THE IRANIAN: She can't help it. She has Alzheimer's.

THE BROTHER: So it doesn't matter where she lives. I have to work. I can't babysit her all day long. I have to be in the store. (IS LOOKING AT A PHOTOGRAPH ON THE COMPUTER SCREEN.) She wants to come here. She's asking me to send money for airplane tickets and a hotel room for two nights in Istanbul.

THE IRANIAN: Who?

THE BROTHER: The one I'm having an online chat with. She wants to come here and marry me.

THE IRANIAN: You're already married. . . . Did you tell her that?

THE BROTHER: She wants me to divorce my wife and marry her.

THE IRANIAN: Did you tell her how old you are?

THE BROTHER: She'll soon see.

THE IRANIAN: You can't go on talking to other women with your wife in the bedroom.

THE BROTHER: She isn't here. She's somewhere else. She's nowhere. I'm here. I'm just forty-seven years old. She's in a place where I can't be with her. She's in a lonely place. I'm here. I'm alive. She isn't. That's not a life.

THE IRANIAN: No.

THE BROTHER: You don't understand. You don't know how it is.

THE IRANIAN: No . . .

THE BROTHER: Well, then, don't judge me.

THE IRANIAN: I'm not judging you. . . . Go to your room.

THE LITTLE ONE: I don't have a room.

THE IRANIAN: Go in there. She shouldn't see this.

THE BROTHER: She already has. She's seen worse things. She has seen her mother disappearing, not recognizing her anymore.

("THE LITTLE ONE" WALKS OVER AND SITS ON THE SOFA, KEEPING VERY STILL.)

THE IRANIAN: Today she drew her first person . . . with eyes and everything . . . arms and legs . . .

THE BROTHER: I need some kind of love. I'm just forty-seven years old. I'm a wreck. I'm taking care of a wreck. I won't last much longer. So, don't say anything.

THE IRANIAN: We've been through much worse.

THE BROTHER: And I've had enough.

(SILENCE)

THE IRANIAN: (STARTS TO PICK UP THE BROKEN PIECES WHILE SHE TALKS.) Maybe it's healthy to break things when you don't know who you are or where you are. (PAUSE) I spoke to Mom today.

THE BROTHER: I did too. Every day. This morning. I carried the woman, or whatever I'm married to, into the bathroom and wiped her ass while my tears were running down my cheeks. After that I spoke to my mom, who keeps crying when she sees her grandchild eating breakfast; and then I walked her over to day care; and then I was in the store for seven hours; and then I drove home to this. There were only seven customers in the store all day. Better than yesterday. Then there were only four.

THE IRANIAN: Mom looked so tired.

THE BROTHER: She's old. She has the right to be tired.

THE IRANIAN: And sick.

THE BROTHER: Yes, what can you do? Are you staying for dinner?

THE IRANIAN: Do you have any food here?

THE BROTHER: I'll get some pizza from downstairs.

THE IRANIAN: She shouldn't eat pizza every day.

THE BROTHER: There are different pizzas, not always the same.

THE IRANIAN: Not every day. (SHORT PAUSE) I'll fix you something.

THE BROTHER: She doesn't recognize me anymore. I'm saying the same thing over and over again, but it doesn't do any good. Bareh knows more than she does.

THE IRANIAN: I'm pregnant.

THE BROTHER: Pregnant? You?

THE IRANIAN: In my fourth month.

THE BROTHER: Who's the father?

THE IRANIAN: A man.

THE BROTHER: A Swede? A Swede? Is he Swedish?

THE IRANIAN: He's a good man. I wanted to have a child with him.

THE BROTHER: What will Dad say?

THE IRANIAN: What could he say?

THE BROTHER: It'll break his heart, if you tell him.

THE IRANIAN: He doesn't have the right to say anything.

THE BROTHER: Why don't you let him die without shame?

(SELUAH COMES IN, STANDS STILL, DOESN'T KNOW WHERE SHE IS.)

THE IRANIAN: This is the only way for me to . . . not forget, not forgive what I've been through . . . but to maybe give me some hope.

THE BROTHER: Well, look how it worked out for me. (SILENCE) She's nineteen. She thinks that I'm twenty-seven.

(SILENCE)

THE IRANIAN: (PICKS UP A BROKEN PICTURE FRAME.) Don't you think this is really serious?

THE BROTHER: No, I don't think so. I've a lot more serious things to worry about than this, like where will I find the money to pay the rent, both for here and the store, and for gas, the Internet, cell phone, electricity, food and other shit. (SILENCE) I need sleep. Just one night I have to get some sleep. I can't take another night with her wandering around screaming and crying.

THE IRANIAN: I can't take her tonight, because I'm working.

THE BROTHER: I'll take her to Yasmin. I'll drive her over there. I can't take it any longer. If it continues like this I'll just kill her.

■

THE BROTHER: Will it be OK?

YASMIN: Yes, I guess it has to. As long as she doesn't wake up Jonah.

THE BROTHER: You have to lock the door.

YASMIN: Last time she woke the whole house up with her knocking, and he got scared. He's afraid of her.

THE BROTHER: Yes, who's not afraid? I've got to get some sleep. You're the only one.

YASMIN: Tonight is OK. I'm up anyway. I feel nauseous lying down. I feel like puking the whole time.

THE BROTHER: Hope it gets better soon.

YASMIN: Otherwise I'll go crazy too.

THE BROTHER: Yes. Sorry, I'm on my way.

YASMIN: Sure.

THE BROTHER: If I could find some kind of home for her it would be easier . . . for me, anyway, but it's taking so long. . . . One of these days . . . well, I don't know. (TO SELUAH) You're staying here tonight. I'll pick you up tomorrow. I'm leaving now, but I'll pick you up tomorrow when you wake up. That's when I'll pick you up.

SELUAH: Who are you?

THE BROTHER: Yes, who am I?

SELUAH: Who is he?

THE BROTHER: Yes, I'm wondering that too.

YASMIN: When are you coming back?

THE BROTHER: Seven-thirty. I have to be in the store at nine. I should open at seven. That's when people are on their way to work. I'm leaving now. (WALKS OUT.)

YASMIN: Come here.

SELUAH: Sarah?

YASMIN: Now you're going to bed. It's time to sleep.

SELUAH: Where's she? Sarah . . .

YASMIN: Sarah isn't here.

SELUAH: Where is she? (CALLS OUT.) Sarah. Sarah.

YASMIN: Sarah is in Iran. She's still there.

SELUAH: Help me, Sarah . . . Sarah!

YASMIN: Be quiet! You have to be quiet when you're here. You've got to be quiet.

SELUAH: Sarah!

YASMIN: If you aren't really quiet the soldiers will come. You see, they'll get angry. Maybe they are standing outside the door. That's why you have to be nice and quiet.

SELUAH: No. (TRIES TO OPEN THE LOCKED DOOR.) Let me go. I want to leave. I want to go to my mommy. I want my mommy. Where is she? Mommy!

■

YASMIN: He's too small for it.

THE SWEDE: He is?

YASMIN: Don't you understand that?

THE SWEDE: But it has support wheels.

YASMIN: He isn't even three years old. He's going to be three. Tomorrow.

THE SWEDE: That's why I bought it.

YASMIN: It'll just be in the way. There's no place for it here.

THE SWEDE: He could try to ride it this summer.

YASMIN: This summer, yes.

(SILENCE)

THE SWEDE: What's wrong?

YASMIN: I don't even have to ask, because I know already what you'll say.

THE SWEDE: Yea . . .

(SILENCE)

YASMIN: So you won't be here tomorrow either?

THE SWEDE: No, I can't.

YASMIN: On his birthday.

THE SWEDE: I really can't.

YASMIN: Well, it's easy for you.

THE SWEDE: Yes, I'm sorry.

YASMIN: Not as sorry as he'll be. He thinks you'll be here, even though he's been deceived so many times. That's all he's been talking about these last days: Daddy is coming, Daddy is coming. . . . It's as much a question as a statement, and I've no more excuses any longer.

THE SWEDE: I'll see him on Saturday when I'm off.

YASMIN: Explain that to him.

THE SWEDE: Yes, I will.

YASMIN: You two could always go to the playground with your other family. (SILENCE) Did you tell her yet? (SILENCE) You haven't told her anything. That's why you haven't answered your phone the whole week.

THE SWEDE: No. But I will. I will.

(SILENCE)

YASMIN: Unless I have to.

THE SWEDE: No, only I can tell her. I'm the one who knows her.

YASMIN: I can't live a lie like this one. I'm falling apart. Everything in my life has become a big lie. My child is a lie. Everything I touch and think about is a lie. It's been three years. No, four years. Four years and just one big lie.

THE SWEDE: Now calm down.

YASMIN: Every single day. (SILENCE) How do you do it? Don't you feel rotten?

THE SWEDE: She's pregnant. She's four months pregnant.

(SILENCE)

YASMIN: I knew it.

THE SWEDE: I can't tell her now. Not yet. She could have another miscarriage. The third one. This morning we saw the doctor and I saw her in there and I heard her heartbeat. The whole room echoed of her heartbeat.

YASMIN: I don't understand how you can live with yourself.

THE SWEDE: What the hell am I to do? I'm trying to keep everything together the best I can. This is not the time for some fucking admission right now. I'm about to go under. I've got bills for forty thousand that I have to pay in the next three days, and I haven't been paid for the job I did a couple of weeks ago, a fancy bathroom restoration that was supposed to pay me twenty thousand dollars. He refuses to pay me. He says he's not approving of my work, and that he has turned to some fucking inspector, who's going to inspect my work; and, as if that wasn't enough, I've got to get enough money together for Nina's birthday on Friday. She wants me to rent the stable, where she goes horseback riding for her and her friends, and take care of the food catering. Fuck, she's only thirteen. She'll be thirteen on Friday. And she stayed overnight with a guy who's eighteen.

YASMIN: This means you're staying with her.

THE SWEDE: No.

YASMIN: Sure it does.

THE SWEDE: No, that's not what it means. It doesn't mean anything. I just need more time. Give me more time. That's what I need. (SILENCE) I couldn't ask her to get rid of it. She wants this child more than anything else.

YASMIN: And you . . . what do you want?

THE SWEDE: I don't know. . . . I want to leave, get away from all the shit and come home to you . . . be with you. But I don't feel I have the right to wish for anything . . . What am I to do? (LISTENS) Is he waking up?

YASMIN: I don't know if I can manage this much longer.

THE SWEDE: Don't talk like that. Not now.

YASMIN: I'm ashamed. (SHORT PAUSE) I feel so humiliated. So dirty. So horribly dirty. (A DOOR OPENS. A LITTLE BOY, THREE YEARS OLD, IS STANDING THERE.) Did you wake up? (SHORT PAUSE) Everything is fine. Mommy is going to bed now. I'll be right there.

THE LITTLE BOY: (IS LOOKING AT THE SWEDE) Daddy?

THE SWEDE: Yes, it's your Daddy.

THE LITTLE BOY: Are you staying? . . . Are you here a long time? . . . The whole time?

■

YASMIN IS STANDING ON THE SUBWAY PLATFORM WITH HER LITTLE BOY. THE SUN IS SHINING BRIGHTLY. ON THE PLATFORM ARE ALSO A NUMBER OF THE CHARACTERS WE HAVE ALREADY MET IN THE PLAY. SHE SAYS SOMETHING TO THE BOY. MAYBE SHE TELLS HIM TO HOLD HER HAND, MAYBE THAT HE MUST HOLD HER HAND. A HALF-DRESSED MAN, HIS FACE INDISTINCTIVE, IS COMING TOWARDS THEM, RUNNING THROUGH THE AUTOMATIC DOORS. HE'S CARRYING A BASEBALL BAT AND WALKS PAST ALL THE PEOPLE WAITING ON THE PLATFORM. THEY MAKE ROOM FOR HIM AS HE PASSES BY. HE LOOKS AT YASMIN AND THE LITTLE BOY, WALKS RIGHT UP TO THEM, LIFTS UP THE BASEBALL BAT AND KILLS THE BOY. THEN HE CONTINUES TO HIT THE AIR AROUND HIM, WHILE THE PEOPLE RUN IN DIFFERENT DIRECTIONS.)

■

(SUNSHINE, VERY STILL, A CEMETERY. WE HEAR YOUNG MEN PLAYING BASKETBALL FURTHER AWAY. YASMIN IS STANDING BY THE OPEN GRAVE WHERE THE CASKET ALREADY HAS BEEN PLACED. "THE SWEDE" IS STANDING ON THE OPPOSITE SIDE, TOGETHER WITH "THE PREGNANT ONE.") (SILENCE) (YASMIN BENDS DOWN AND DROPS A STUFFED ANIMAL INTO THE GRAVE. THEY ALL REMAIN THERE FOR A WHILE LONGER. YASMIN WALKS AROUND THE GRAVE AND GOES UP TO THE PREGNANT WOMAN.)

THE PREGNANT ONE: I didn't know you existed.

YASMIN: Thank you for coming.

THE PREGNANT ONE: Yes, I didn't know . . .

YASMIN: No.

(SILENCE)

THE PREGNANT ONE: Can I . . .

YASMIN: No.

THE PREGNANT ONE: But you knew . . .

YASMIN: Yes, for three years.

THE PREGNANT ONE: Three years?

YASMIN: Jonah was three years old.

(SILENCE)

THE PREGNANT ONE: Three years old?

YASMIN: He'll always be three years old.

THE PREGNANT ONE: I never knew anything . . .

YASMIN: No.

THE PREGNANT ONE: But it doesn't matter . . . I've felt that there . . . (SILENCE) No, I can't . . . I'm sorry . . . I can't. (TURNS AROUND AND LEAVES.)

(SILENCE)

THE SWEDE: I want to take you home.

YASMIN: Where?

THE SWEDE: Well, just go home.

■

("THE PREGNANT ONE" IS AT HOME WITH HER MOTHER. "THE MOTHER OF THE PREGNANT ONE," AROUND FIFTY-THREE YEARS OLD, IS VERY ILL WITH CANCER; NOT LONG TO LIVE. SHE DOES NOT WANT TO STAY IN THE HOSPITAL. SHE WANTS TO DIE AT HOME. WHITNEY HOUSTON MUSIC IS PLAYING.)

THE MOTHER OF THE PREGNANT ONE: (LOUDLY) It smells like cancer when she comes.

THE PREGNANT ONE: What did you say? I didn't hear you.

THE MOTHER OF THE PREGNANT ONE: The nurse—when she comes here—that's what she says: It smells like cancer here.

THE PREGNANT ONE: Oh, that one, yes.

THE MOTHER OF THE PREGNANT ONE: That's her sense of humor. I guess that's good. You have to laugh a little, however horrible it is. (LISTENS TO THE MUSIC, SINGS ALONG.) This is the one I want to . . .

THE PREGNANT ONE: Yes, I know. You've told me already.

THE MOTHER OF THE PREGNANT ONE: Do you remember it? We always played it. You feel good listening to it . . . but maybe there should be something to make people cry. Otherwise I guess they won't cry.

THE PREGNANT ONE: Did I give it to you?

THE MOTHER OF THE PREGNANT ONE: That one? You gave it to me? No, Bertil gave it to me. . . . No, not Bertil, Sam. I guess it was Sam. He brought it to me.

THE PREGNANT ONE: No, I was the one who bought it. Used my first money. You got it on my birthday. My first salary. And I bought it because I knew you liked it.

THE MOTHER OF THE PREGNANT ONE: Yes, but I don't remember.

THE PREGNANT ONE: I was fourteen years old. I was cleaning at the Sheraton. Cleaning the rooms.

THE MOTHER OF THE PREGNANT ONE: Yes, but that was a long time ago.

THE PREGNANT ONE: Yes, I was fourteen.

THE MOTHER OF THE PREGNANT ONE: Is it that old, is it that long ago? . . . How old was I then?

THE PREGNANT ONE: I had just met Johnny.

THE MOTHER OF THE PREGNANT ONE: Oh, him, yes, that fucking psychopath. I guess he's dead by now.

THE PREGNANT ONE: He got a tattoo with my name after just one month.

THE MOTHER OF THE PREGNANT ONE: I guess he's not with us anymore, we hope.

THE PREGNANT ONE: I didn't even like him, but he was eighteen years old, so you felt kind of honored to be his girl. But then we moved away and I didn't see him again.

THE MOTHER OF THE PREGNANT ONE: Well anyway, that's the one I want at the funeral. And it should be very loud.

THE PREGNANT ONE: You'll have it, I promise.

THE MOTHER OF THE PREGNANT ONE: Did you get everything?

THE PREGNANT ONE: Yes.

THE MOTHER OF THE PREGNANT ONE: Did you write it down? And no yellow flowers, and no pink ones either.

THE PREGNANT ONE: No.

THE MOTHER OF THE PREGNANT ONE: It should be worthy . . . and respectful.

THE PREGNANT ONE: Yes, Mom.

THE MOTHER OF THE PREGNANT ONE: Yes, it is what it is. (SILENCE) You only die once . . . I hope. . . . So, you know, you want it to look good.

THE PREGNANT ONE: What about all your men?

THE MOTHER OF THE PREGNANT ONE: Oh, those guys. . . . Where are they?

THE PREGNANT ONE: Would you like any of them to be there?

THE MOTHER OF THE PREGNANT ONE: No. No one. Just you and Tony. If he can make it. You never know where he is. And maybe one of the dogs. They'll miss me, anyway. They are the ones I worry about.

THE PREGNANT ONE: You don't think that I'll miss you?

THE MOTHER OF THE PREGNANT ONE: Well, I hope so. Anyway, we know how it will end. I might have a couple of months left, if I'm lucky . . . or unlucky. Depends on how you look at it. Then everything will be fine. As long as I get enough morphine, to give me some happiness. That they have promised. I don't want to be alone somewhere in a corner, screaming my head off, without getting any help.

THE PREGNANT ONE: "I Will Survive" . . . shouldn't that one be part of it?

THE MOTHER OF THE PREGNANT ONE: Yes, that one. "I Will Survive." That one should be played as loud as anything. Then one might start dancing again. How the hell could I forget that one? Those were the best times of my life. (THEY BOTH START TO SING "I WILL SURVIVE.") (AFTER A WHILE) Well, they should see me now . . .

THE PREGNANT ONE: You look fine . . . you look younger somehow.

THE MOTHER OF THE PREGNANT ONE: I do?

THE PREGNANT ONE: Yes . . . like a girl.

THE MOTHER OF THE PREGNANT ONE: Yes, what good does that do me? (SHORT PAUSE) Take whatever you want. . . . It is what it is. There must be something here for you to sell.

THE PREGNANT ONE: I don't have room for any more stuff.

THE MOTHER OF THE PREGNANT ONE: It's just crap anyway.

THE PREGNANT ONE: I don't even know if I can stay in my apartment. . . . I have to pay last month's rent in two weeks, but I hardly have enough for food . . . if I don't get that job.

THE MOTHER OF THE PREGNANT ONE: There are photographs . . . you'd want them, wouldn't you? (SHORT PAUSE) But I don't know where they are. I haven't had the strength to look for them.

∎

THE SWEDE: May I come in?

THE PREGNANT ONE: Sure. (SILENCE) Come in.

THE SWEDE: Yes . . . thank you. (SHORT PAUSE) Should I take them off?

THE PREGNANT ONE: Take off what?

THE SWEDE: The shoes. My shoes.

THE PREGNANT ONE: No. You don't have to.

THE SWEDE: But they're dirty. I've been working in an attic, converting it into an apartment. Putting down flooring. Haven't had a chance to change. (TAKES HIS SHOES OFF.) I'll put them here.

THE PREGNANT ONE: OK. (SILENCE) Do you want something to eat?

THE SWEDE: No, thanks.

THE PREGNANT ONE: Good. Because I don't have anything.

THE SWEDE: How's it going?

THE PREGNANT ONE: I have tea and crackers.

THE SWEDE: No, thanks, it's fine. . . . (SHORT PAUSE) How's it going?

THE PREGNANT ONE: What?

THE SWEDE: Well, with everything?

THE PREGNANT ONE: She's getting bigger . . . if that's what you mean. That's what she's doing. For nine months.

THE SWEDE: Yes. (SILENCE) What about the job . . . that you tried to get?

THE PREGNANT ONE: The job?

THE SWEDE: Yes, the one you were trying to get.

THE PREGNANT ONE: Which one? I don't remember all the jobs I've tried to get.

THE SWEDE: I don't know which one.

THE PREGNANT ONE: Me neither. There must be at least thirty.

THE SWEDE: I know . . . the dog shelter. Right?

THE PREGNANT ONE: Oh, that one.

THE SWEDE: You worked there before. Didn't they have anything?

THE PREGNANT ONE: No.

THE SWEDE: I see. OK.

THE PREGNANT ONE: Not right now. They can't promise anything. They don't even have money to keep some of the ones working there

THE SWEDE: No, it's tough. It's tough everywhere.

THE PREGNANT ONE: Just as well I didn't get it. I keep crying the whole time, seeing the poor dogs nobody wants . . . just waiting there for someone to come and take care of them.

THE SWEDE: Yes. (SILENCE) I heard you saw Yasmin.

THE PREGNANT ONE: Really.

THE SWEDE: Yes . . . why?

THE PREGNANT ONE: She called me. She wanted to see me.

THE SWEDE: Anything special?

THE PREGNANT ONE: She called and asked if we could meet.

THE SWEDE: Yes.

THE PREGNANT ONE: Yes, I couldn't say no.

THE SWEDE: No.

(SILENCE)

THE PREGNANT ONE: I couldn't say no when she asked.

THE SWEDE: No, maybe . . . maybe . . .

(SILENCE)

THE PREGNANT ONE: So, you've moved in with her.

THE SWEDE: Is that what she said?

THE PREGNANT ONE: Yes.

THE SWEDE: Yes. . . . Sometimes.

THE PREGNANT ONE: Really. (SILENCE) She said that that was what you had in mind the whole time.

THE SWEDE: No, that's not true.

THE PREGNANT ONE: Since she knew. I didn't know anything. I didn't know she existed.

THE SWEDE: Yes, but we . . . she and I, we've tried to break up the whole time . . . from the beginning; left each other and tried that, but then we've come together again, even though . . . just a lot of fighting, and we don't suit each other, we're completely different, as different as one can get; but it doesn't help, it's still impossible to break apart. Hell, it's as if it was something else, as if a higher power ruled over us. Every time I've sworn that it would be the last time, this time it's over, now I can't any longer, but . . . hell, I don't even know if I like her; sometimes I don't think I do because we don't feel the same way about anything we do or what we like. There aren't two people who are more unlike each other; we're like oil and water. . . . And when I met you and fell in love with you it was because you were so completely different from her. And I thought it was over, I thought I was getting my life straightened out and was able to work normally again, but then we happened to end up in the same subway train, same cabin, and I tried not to look at her, but I knew she was standing there. And when I got off she followed me . . . for several blocks. . . . If we didn't have the boy, everything would be so much simpler. I've had to stay in contact with her, because since it's . . . since he was my little guy . . . and now it's like he's here even more than when he was alive in some way. (SHORT PAUSE) It's strange, when I hear what she tells friends about me it's completely different than what she tells me, what she calls me. . . . It's a totally different person she's talking about . . . than what she gives off to me. (SHORT PAUSE) I don't know what it is. It's like an illness.

THE PREGNANT ONE: She wants my child.

THE SWEDE: What?

THE PREGNANT ONE: This one. She says it's hers.

■

THE SWEDE IS WORKING IN AN ATHLETIC COMPLEX WITH A BIG SWIMMING POOL, PUTTING UP TILES ON A WALL. THERE ARE STRINGS HANGING IN FRONT OF THE NAKED WALL. HE IS PUTTING UP ONE TILE AFTER ANOTHER. WE HEAR SOUNDS FROM LOUD, HAPPY CHILDREN, A LOT OF NOISE. A MIDDLE-AGED MAN IS WALKING THROUGH THE ROOM WHERE THE SWEDE IS WORKING, WHISTLING NERVOUSLY. THE MIDDLE-AGED MAN IS CARRYING SOMETHING THAT LOOKS LIKE A BIG, HARD COVER FOR A GOLF CLUB.)

TWO GUARDS: (RUNNING TRYING TO CATCH HIM.) Hey, stop! You aren't allowed in here! You can't go in there! The swim hall is booked for school kids!

THE SECOND GUARD: It's booked up today . . . fucking idiot . . .

THE FIRST GUARD: Better call the police.

THE SECOND GUARD: We did, Sonja called.

THE FIRST GUARD: He's not allowed in there.

THE SECOND GUARD: No. Hello, hello, stop!

THE SWEDE: He went that way. . . . What's going on?

THE FIRST GUARD: They are having a swim meet today . . . and then this guy shows up.

THE SWEDE: Yes, I saw that he was fully dressed.

(WE HEAR SOUNDS OF GUNFIRE AND SCREAMS. THE LAUGHTER STOPS.)

■

(IN A BAR)

THE FIRST GUARD: No, fuck I . . .

THE SECOND GUARD: Yea.

THE FIRST GUARD: I don't know . . . I called Lena, I talked to her . . .

THE SECOND GUARD: Yes. (SHORT PAUSE) It's good to talk.

THE FIRST GUARD: Yes, she's good to talk to, she's smart.

THE SECOND GUARD: There were seven . . .

THE FIRST GUARD: Yes . . .

THE SECOND GUARD: And then he killed himself.

THE FIRST GUARD: Yes, the easy way out.

THE SECOND GUARD: Yes, much too easy.

THE FIRST GUARD: I saw something was up with him. I saw it when he came in.

THE SECOND GUARD: Sure thing, it was obvious.

THE FIRST GUARD: I was just picking up a cup of coffee. That's when he came in through the door. And then when I saw him I said that there was no fucking way he was allowed in today. The swim hall is booked for the school kids today, a swim meet . . .

THE SECOND GUARD: Yes.

THE FIRST GUARD: There were all the trophies standing there, that they were going to get.

THE SECOND GUARD: It happened so fucking fast.

THE FIRST GUARD: I didn't get it . . . didn't get what was going on until it happened . . . was over.

THE SECOND GUARD: No . . . did you see him when he died?

THE FIRST GUARD: Sure as hell I did. I saw how he put it in his mouth and fired. . . . But then I don't remember anything. What happened?

THE SECOND GUARD: Well, he fell down. Dead.

THE FIRST GUARD: Did he fall into the pool?

THE SECOND GUARD: No, he was on the edge of the pool. He was still there when the police came. I jumped into the pool with clothes and everything and tried to be of some help.

THE FIRST GUARD: Sorry, I can't stay here.

THE SECOND GUARD: No.

THE FIRST GUARD: I've got to go.

THE SECOND GUARD: Yes. . . . It could've been us. It could just as well have been us.

THE FIRST GUARD: Yes, sure.

THE SECOND GUARD: Sonja had to go to the ER.

THE FIRST GUARD: Yes.

THE SECOND GUARD: Can't figure out what kind of "sicko" he was. (SHORT PAUSE) But we'll probably never know.

THE FIRST GUARD: No . . .

THE SECOND GUARD: I've got kids myself. They have been swimming in that pool their whole lives. Since they were about two, three years old. Several times a month. Almost every Friday. That was the first thing I thought about. The first thing I thought was that Curt and Nina were there today. That was my first thought. Curt and Nina. But they're in daycare. It was only ten a.m. I called Helen and checked on them, and she said they were at the daycare place. She had left them there at eight-thirty. She had dropped off a paper to get some tax credit or something.

THE END

3.31.93.*

* NOTE: In this version of 3.31.93., which is based on the manuscript prepared for the world premiere at the Stockholm City Theater by its director, Sofia Jupither, there are some scenes that have been omitted while other scenes have changed position in relationship to the original published Swedish play.

Characters

(In Order of Appearance)

- A: Young man (22-23)
- B: Young woman (20-22)
- I: Man (30-35)
- J: Woman (27-33)
- C: Man (38-45) father of Ee
- D: Woman (35-45)
- E: Young woman (20-25) mother of Ee
- F: Woman (48-58) mother of E / Grandmother of Ee
- L: Man (45-55) father of K's child
- K: Woman (35-45)
- O: Man (65-70) husband of P
- P: Woman (60-68)
- R: Woman (60-70) Mother of W
- G: Man (50-70)
- S: Man (65-75)
- X: Woman (30-40) wife of Y
- Y: Man (30-40) stroke victim
- N: Woman (50-60) nurse
- T: Man (35-45) son of O and P, brother of H
- W: Man (34-40) son of R
- H: Man (35-45) son of O and P, brother of T
- Q: Man (55-65) father of Y
- V: Man (45-55)
- U: Woman (23-26) daughter of V
- Young Girl's Voice (8-10)
- Ee: Daughter of E (5-7)
- OO: Man (35-45) boyfriend of K

ACT 1

DARKNESS.
LIGHT.

1.

A: Where is she?

B: Who?

A: You know. (PAUSE) Where's she now?

B: Now?

A: Yea, she isn't here.

B: She's dead. She died.

A: Yea, I know. . . .

B: She died.

A: But where's she now? She must be somewhere.

B: They took her away. I don't know where they took her. She's dead.

A: Yes, I know.

B: Yes. (PAUSE) So she can't be here.

A: No, of course not.

B: My thumb has cracks in it.

A: It does? (PAUSE) When will they let you go home?

B: Go?

A: Yes, home.

B: Well, not today anyway.

A: I know, but when?

B: I don't know.

A: You are coming home soon, aren't you?

B: I'm thirsty. I want something to drink.

A: What do you want?

B: Anything.

A: Aha.

B: Could you get it for me?

A: Where?

B: A Coke or something, from the vending machine out there. The one out there.

A: Oh, there.

B: Hurry up.

A: Do you have any money, any change?

B: How could I have any money? Don't you have any?

A: Only my debit card.

B: So go and get some then.

A: Yes, but I don't know if it'll work. I don't know if there's anything there yet. There might not be anything until Monday. (SILENCE) Tell me something. (PAUSE) Please tell me.

B: What?

A: Did you see her? (PAUSE) Did you see her?

B: They wanted me to.

A: What did she look like?

B: What she looked like?

A: Yes.

B: There wasn't much to see.

A: Did she look like someone?

B: Who?

A: Her?

B: You?

A: Yes, or . . . who else?

B: She was dead. She looked dead. As if she was sleeping.

A: Did she look like somebody else?

DARKNESS.
LIGHT.

2.

I: Are you awake?

J: Awake?

I: Yes.

J: I wasn't sleeping.

I: No, I . . . I didn't know. . . . It looked like, as if you . . .

J: Did you sleep?

I: No, not very well . . . maybe a few hours . . . I guess. (SILENCE) I came home pretty late. (SILENCE) So . . . (SILENCE) It's snowing again. Outside. (SILENCE) I could hardly get the car out of the snow-drift this morning. It's been snowing all night. I couldn't find our . . . when I came outside this morning. I didn't recognize where I was. I didn't know where I was. That's how much snow there was. But finally I found it. (SILENCE) Are you tired?

J: No.

I: Did you get a good breakfast this morning?

J: Breakfast?

I: Yes . . . I'll sit here.

J: What did you say? What are you talking about?

I: I said . . . I'll sit here. Over here. (SILENCE)

J: What are you doing?

I: I thought I'd show you . . . Do you want to see?

J: No.

I: But it's a nice picture. . . . She looks so . . .

J: Don't you get it, that I don't want to see it.

I: But she looks so peaceful . . . as if she . . .

J: Was alive.

I: No, was asleep. Asleep . . . as if she was sleeping.

J: I don't want to see anything.

I: (QUIETLY) No . . . but you wanted me to take a picture.

J: How can you even think I want to see her?

I: No, no. I . . . I understand.

DARKNESS.
LIGHT.

3.

C: Can I sit here? ("D" DOESN'T ANSWER. DOESN'T LOOK UP.) Here. On this chair?

D: Yes.

C: I can sit here? (HE SITS DOWN. LOOKS AT HER. IS SITTING STILL. IS BENT OVER, AS IF HE WAS VERY COLD. TRIES TO AVOID LOOKING AT HER, BUT CAN'T RESIST. WE DON'T KNOW IF SHE IS AWARE OF HIM LOOKING AT HER, OR IF SHE IS TRYING TO AVOID HIM.) (SILENCE) (HE IS TRYING TO BEHAVE AS IF HE WAS WAITING FOR SOMEONE.) Yes, I wonder if . . . (SILENCE) How are you? Is it . . . (D DOESN'T REACT.) Yes, sorry, it wasn't . . . but has . . . is there someone who has . . . (D IS ABOUT TO STAND UP. C PUTS HIS HAND ON HERS AND THEN PULLS IT QUICKLY AWAY.) Wait. (SILENCE) I don't want to . . . Well, I'm sorry, I didn't mean . . . I didn't mean to touch you.

D: What?

C: I didn't mean to. I just thought . . . you looked like something had happened to you, but . . .

D: No.

C: No.

D: What?

C: I don't know.

D: No.

C: No. (PAUSE) Is there someone who has . . .

D: No.

C: Yes, what's there to do?

D: I don't know.

C: No. (SILENCE) I've never . . . I don't usually . . . When I saw you today . . . I usually see you . . . here. But I usually don't . . . it's never happened before, as far as I remember anyway, but it felt like I had to talk to you, come here and sit down and tell you something. To make myself aware to you. As if I'd waited for you my whole life.

D: No.

C: No, I know. (PAUSE) I dreamt about you a couple of weeks ago. Yes, I'm sorry, but in my dream we were sitting here, across from each other, in here, in the dark, without saying a word. Then you told me that your husband had committed suicide, had jumped in front of a subway train.

DARKNESS.
LIGHT.

4.

E: Is that me?

F: I think so.

E: Who else could it be?

F: It must be.

E: Even though I didn't look like that.

F: You didn't?

(SILENCE)

E: You look so young.

F: I was young then. (PAUSE) It's hard to imagine. (SILENCE)

(THEY ARE WATCHING A BLACK AND WHITE 8-MILLIMETER FILM.)

E: And him?

F: Yes.

E: Is that him?

(SILENCE)

F: Yes. That's him.

E: He was good looking.

F: You think so.

E: In a way . . . (SILENCE) We look alike.

F: Who?

E: You and me. We look so much alike.

F: Why wouldn't we?

E: The same . . . (SILENCE) Is it a party?

F: Yes, it looks like it. There are balloons. It's your birthday.

E: How old do you think?

F: Well . . .

E: How old was I there . . . in the film?

F: Yes, how old could you've been there?

E: Five . . . six?

F: Yes, I think it's your sixth birthday. When you turned six years old.

E: Six years old?

F: Yes, I think so.

E: Where is it?

F: I don't know. I don't remember.

E: You don't?

F: No, it . . .

E: Since he's there too.

F: Yes, I guess it must've been the last summer. . . . We had rented a little house. I don't remember where. (SILENCE) I don't remember.

E: No.

F: I'm sorry but I haven't seen these films before. It was so long ago. (SILENCE) I can't remember everything.

E: You were so cute.

F: You think so?

E: Yes.

F: No, it . . .

E: In that dress.

(SILENCE)

F: Yes, I remember the dress. That was the first time I wore it. It was too big.

DARKNESS.
LIGHT.

5.

L: Well, then . . .

(SILENCE)

K: What?

L: Did she fall asleep?

K: Yes, I hope so.

L: Yes. . . . She was tired.

K: Not as tired as I am.

L: No. I understand.

K: I don't know how I'm going to make it.

L: No.

K: I'm the one taking at least eighty-five percent responsibility for her, if not more.

L: Yes, I know.

K: What good does that do?

L: What?

K: That you know. (SILENCE) Are you leaving now?

L: Yes, I am. (SHORT PAUSE) That's what we had decided.

K: Yes, I guess we did.

L: Yes?

K: No, it's fine. I can't take it much longer.

L: No, I know.

K: Yea.

L: Me neither. (SILENCE) Well . . . where did I put my scarf?

K: I don't know.

L: It's not here.

K: Where are you going?

L: Well, home.

K: Home?

L: Where else would I go?

K: Isn't this your home?

L: To my sister.

K: So you have a new home.

L: I mean, I'm going home to them. (SILENCE) For now anyway. (SILENCE) Until I find something.

K: Sure.

L: It's not going to be easy, but . . .

K: No.

L: No, not easy at all. (SILENCE) See you tomorrow.

K: Tomorrow?

L: I'm supposed to pick her up tomorrow. That's what we said.

K: Yes, that's right.

L: Yes . . . What time? What time should I pick her up?

K: Why don't we talk about it later.

L: Sure we can.

K: Yes.

(SILENCE)

L: I don't understand that you don't care about me.

K: What did you say?

L: I don't understand that you don't care about me.

DARKNESS.
LIGHT.

6.

O: Yes, now there's plenty of time.

P: There is?

O: For what?

P: You tell me.

O: Now that there isn't that much time left, then there's plenty of time.

P: Why do you put on a suit every day?

O: What else should I do?

P: Now that you can do whatever you want. Now that you don't have to do that.

O: Why wouldn't I? They should be used . . . before it's too late.

P: Too late?

O: Too late to be wearing them.

P: You could wear whatever you want.

O: Yes, but I don't want to. (SILENCE) What are we doing today?

P: I don't know what you're doing, but I'm going to the Salvation Army. I'm working in the café today. Since it's Thursday.

O: If only we had our children . . .

P: But we do, two of them.

O: Yes, but where are they?

P: They have their own lives. Just like everybody else.

O: Shouldn't they visit here now and then? Soon enough we won't be around. (SILENCE)

P: Why don't you read a book or something?

O: Why would I do that? (SILENCE)

DARKNESS.
LIGHT.

7.

(R WALKS PAST THEM DRESSED IN HOSPITAL GARB, AND CONTINUES TOWARDS THE DOOR. IT IS LOCKED. SHE STANDS THERE, REMAINS STANDING QUIETLY. G COMES IN HOLDING A BANANA, WHICH HE HAS TIED WITH A WHITE STRING. HE SITS DOWN, IS SITTING PATTING HIS BANANA. S IS SITTING, STARING WITH AN EMPTY LOOK.)

S: Are you going to eat it?

G: Eat it?

S: Yes.

G: No.

(SILENCE)

S: Why are you patting it?

G: Why?

S: Yes. The way you're doing it.

G: I have to take care of the darn cat.

R: Is it locked?

J: Yes, can't you see that is?

R: Why?

J: Because it is . . .

R: I don't want to go outside. (SILENCE) Why do they lock the door?

J: Yes, why do they do that?

DARKNESS.
LIGHT.

8.

X: So now we're home. (WHEELS IN Y WHO'S SITTING IN THE WHEEL CHAIR.) I'm just going to . . . Everything OK? (Y IS TRYING TO TURN AROUND TO LOOK AT HER. IT IS AS IF HE WANTED TO SAY: WHAT? HOW THE HELL COULD IT BE OK?) Now you're home. (Y SHUTS HIS EYES.) Isn't it nice? (Y LOOKS LIKE HE WAS GOING TO SAY "NICE?") (SILENCE) I've got to sit down. (SHORT PAUSE) (Y IS TRYING TO MOVE, TO BREAK HIS PARALYZING FEELING. HE HAS BEEN SITTING WITH HIS HEAD FACED DOWN. HE LOOKS WORRIED.) Do you want me to turn you around? Is that what you want? (STANDS UP SLOWLY, WALKS UP TO HIM, TURNS THE WHEEL CHAIR SO THAT HE CAN LOOK AT HER WHEN SHE SITS DOWN AGAIN. SHE NOTICES THE PAIN IN HIS

EYES, WHICH LOOKS LIKE HATRED.) (SILENCE) Well . . . Do you want to listen to some music? (PAUSE) Maybe later. (SHORT PAUSE) I'm going to take my coat off. (STILL SITTING WHERE SHE WAS.) Did we bring everything home? (SHORT PAUSE) It's like a whole book . . . a Bible for the sick . . . but maybe it's good to have . . . everything in one place. (SILENCE) (AGAIN Y IS CLOSING HIS EYES.) How does it feel to be home? (SHORT PAUSE) John? (SHORT PAUSE) John? (Y DOESN'T LOOK AT HER.) (SHORT PAUSE) Why don't you look at me? (SILENCE) How are you? No, sorry. (SHORT PAUSE) Do you want me to take your coat? (SHORT PAUSE) You can't keep your coat on inside. (STANDS UP, WALKS UP TO HIM, REMOVES HIS COAT, WHICH IS DIFFICULT AND PAINFUL, THEN SHE WALKS OUT WITH THE COAT WHILE HE REMAINS IN THE UNCOMFORTABLE POSITION HE ENDED UP IN, ALMOST LIKE NAILED TO THE CROSS. SHE COMES BACK, NOTICES HIS POSITION, PUSHES HIS BODY BACK IN THE CHAIR SO THAT HE AGAIN IS SITTING UPRIGHT.) (SILENCE) (X REMAINS STANDING WHERE SHE IS.) Do you want something to eat? (SILENCE) (SHORT PAUSE) So you don't want anything?

Y: (MAKES A SOUND.)

X: No. . . . I'll get some music going . . . . Well . . .

Y: (MAKES AN EVEN STRONGER SOUND.)

X: You don't want music? Why not? (SILENCE) No, no. The music will always be there. There will always be music. I haven't listened to music for a long time either . . . haven't felt like it really . . . well, I don't know. (SHORT PAUSE) I really haven't played anything since you got sick. (SILENCE) John. Your dad, I wanted to tell you . . . he called this morning before I went to pick you up. He asked if he could come and help us pick you up in his car. I told him I'd rather do it myself. If we needed it, they would give us help there. (SHORT PAUSE) He sent his best. He asked if he could visit us tonight, once you were home . . . but I thought it would be better if he came another day. Since this is the first evening you're home.

Y: (SAYS SOMETHING, BUT IT CAN'T BE UNDERSTOOD.)

X: What did you say?

Y: (TRIES AGAIN, MAKING A SOUND.)

X: I don't understand. . . . I don't understand what you're saying. (SHORT PAUSE, TRIES NOT TO SHOW HER FEELINGS TOWARDS HIS GARBLE.) What do you want? Do you want something? (SHORT PAUSE) What?

Y: (TRIES AGAIN, MAKING A SOUND.)

X: What? (SHORT PAUSE) Try.

Y: (TRIES AGAIN, AS IF HE WAS SCREAMING.)

X: Yes, but . . . it doesn't help me. Point. Point to what you want. (SILENCE) (Y SINKS BACK IN THE CHAIR.) I don't know what you want. I don't understand. I'm sorry, but I don't understand. (SILENCE) (THEN SHE FOLLOWS HIS EYES IN THE DIRECTION OF A LADDER LEANING AGAINST THE WALL BEHIND HER.) Yes, he helped me with the painting. It's his ladder. He used it when he did the ceiling. Don't you see that it's freshly painted? He was here one day and did the painting.

DARKNESS.
LIGHT.

9.

N: What did you want?

R: What?

N: You called me.

R: I did?

N: Yes.

R: Why?

(SILENCE)

N: What did you want?

R: Something to drink.

N: Drink? You have water over there.

R: No, not water. Vodka.

N: Vodka?

R: Yes.

N: No. (SHORT PAUSE)

R: Yes, that's what I want. (SHORT PAUSE) Now.

N: No, that's . . .

R: Dear . . . (SHORT PAUSE) They're eating me up.

N: Yes, I know.

R: They've eaten my face.

N: I know.

R: That's my right. It's my . . . it's my money.

N: Don't think about that now.

R: No.

N: Try to think about something else. Something nice.

R: That's the only thing I can think about, that's nice.

N: You know we don't have booze here. You know you'll never be able to drink anymore alcohol again, ever. Not if you want to live.

R: But I'm dying.

N: We all are. (SILENCE)

R: Three months, he said . . .

N: You aren't going to die today anyway.

R: I wish . . . Since one is dying, one should get what one wants. I don't know where they are.

N: What are you talking about?

R: The hands. My hands.

DARKNESS.
LIGHT.

10.

QUIET LIGHT.

S: What did you say?

T: How are things?

S: How are things?

T: Yes, I just wanted to . . .

S: Well, it's not good.

T: No . . . I understand.

S: You do?

T: Yes, since you're . . . since you're here. Then . . .

S: How's it possible to say that everything's good. It's bad. It would be better without these fucking shakes in my hands the whole time, but it'll never be good again. It's the medications I take, that make me shake from morning to night, even when I'm asleep. I feel like nailing them to the wall in order to get some peace and quiet.

T: What kind of medications?

S: I don't know. I take them because I have emphysema.

T: I see.

S: Even though it's been ten years since I stopped.

T: Seems like a terrible illness.

S: You see the young girls standing outside smoking, and you feel like telling them to stub out the cigarettes before it's too late, but they couldn't possibly imagine that they might end up like this. They can't even imagine what next year will be like.

T: No, I'm sure they don't.

(SILENCE)

S: Are you a minister or something?

T: Yes, I'm a lay minister.

S: Is that the same as a minister?

T: Yes, almost . . . we basically do the same things.

S: Same God I guess.

T: Yes, indeed. I started studying to become a minister a couple of years ago. Before that I was an actor. I haven't graduated yet.

S: So, what do you want with me?

T: Well, I just wanted to sit here and talk to you for a little while.

S: About what?

T: Anything. There's nothing . . .

S: You're the one who came to see me.

T: I know.

S: I want to go home. Period.

T: We could just sit here without talking . . . for a while.

S: I don't want you to sit here without talking.

T: No . . .

S: What did your parents do?

T: My parents?

S: Your Dad . . . what did he do?

T: Well, he . . .

S: He did something, didn't he?

T: He, well, it . . . I don't know if . . .

S: Is it hard to talk about?

T: No, it's not. Not at all. It's just that . . .

S: Did he beat you?

T: Sorry? Beat me?

S: You were beaten, weren't you?

T: No, I wasn't. No, not at all. He was a very . . .

S: You screamed until you fainted. You, yourself had to go and get the whip, and then put your ass up in the air.

T: No, he worked for AstraZeneca in the financial department.

DARKNESS.
LIGHT.

11.

(W IS SITTING ON A BENCH IN A SUBWAY STATION. HE LOOKS CALM AND RELAXED. BY HIS SIDE HE HAS A BRIEFCASE, WHICH IS OPEN. HE IS PICKING UP ONE PIECE OF PAPER AFTER ANOTHER AND TEARS THEM UP WITHOUT SAYING A WORD. B SITS DOWN BESIDE HIM.)

W: Sorry. Let me get it out of your way.

B: No problem. There's room.

W: Yes, but . . . (COLLECTS WHAT HE CAN GRAB.) I'll put the papers here instead. Nothing important. (SILENCE) Are you on your way home?

B: Who? Me?

W: Yes.

B: No.

W: I am.

B: Aha.

(SILENCE)

W: I was going to visit my mom. She's in the hospital up there. But I changed my mind. I don't even know if she would recognize me. I haven't seen her in nine years, but they called and said that she doesn't have very long to live. She's an alcoholic. She has drunk herself to death. That's what she wanted. You can't talk to someone who doesn't want anything but that. She never drank when I was little, before my dad left us. Not really after that either. I've no memories of her as an alcoholic, no bad memories. She started drinking just a few years ago, with the purpose of drinking herself to death. That's what she has been waiting for. She must have had an enormous willpower, since she managed to stay sober for so many years, until I moved away from home and she was left all alone.

B: That's my train.

W: Yes . . . catch it.

B: Yes.

W: Take care. . . . Hope everything will work out for you. (SILENCE) I feel good about not visiting her. It feels good. A relief, really. I usually don't do what I really want. I don't know if she would even recognize me.

I: Sorry?

W: Well, I don't know if she would recognize me. Maybe she would. In some way. Since I am her child, her only child.

I: Aha.

(SILENCE)

W: The train just left.

I: I noticed.

W: But the next one will soon be here.

I: Yes, in seven minutes.

W: Seven minutes?

I: Yes, that's what it says . . . up there, on the board.

W: Yes, that's right. Seven minutes.

I: If the board can be trusted.

W: Is that it?

I: Sorry?

W: Is that it? Just seven minutes to go?

I: Yes . . . now it's six.

W: Still less. Well, the less the better.

I: Yesterday it didn't come for over thirty minutes.

W: Here?

I: Yes, but that was yesterday. Today I don't know, but it doesn't say anything. Five.

W: Five?

I: Now it's just five.

W: It is . . . there are so few people here.

I: Now, yes. Most people are home already, I guess.

W: I hope so. I'm going home as well.

I: Yes, it . . .

W: I am. In a way. I'm looking forward to it. (REMOVES HIS WATCH.) Do you want it?

I: What?

W: Take it.

I: The watch?

W: I bought it in New York. Ten years ago. It's still working. Take it.

I: I have one already, in my cell phone.

W: Well, then I'll put it here.

I: Sure. (STANDS UP.)

W: Maybe there's someone . . . Are you leaving?

I: Yes, I guess that's . . .

W: The train isn't here yet. (SHORT PAUSE) One can hear when it's coming, I guess?

DARKNESS.
LIGHT.

12.

R: Who are you?

T: We've met before. Don't you remember? (TAKES HER HAND.)

R: No.

T: I usually pay you a visit . . . sit down and talk a little . . . about all kinds of things. (SHORT PAUSE) I talk to you. (SHORT PAUSE) We talked for a long time last week. You probably remember.

R: Yes.

T: We talked about your marriage and your son. (SHORT PAUSE) Have you heard anything from him?

R: No.

T: They all have so much going on . . .

R: I have nothing.

T: No, sometimes we have to adjust to . . . what we can't change . . . and trust in God. It might be that what seems so difficult is just a way to . . . (PAUSE) I can see that you're tired, very tired really, so I won't stay with you much longer. (LETS GO OF HER HAND, THEN PATS IT LIGHTLY.)

R: Where is he?

T: Why don't you rest for a while? (STANDS UP.) You'll see, everything will . . .

R: He's gone. He just disappeared.

DARKNESS.
LIGHT.

13.

P: Is that you?

H: Yes it is.

P: Aha.

(SILENCE)

H: May I come in, or should I stay here?

O: Are you here?

H: I just wanted to see if you have . . .

P: Did something happen?

H: Would that be the only reason?

P: What?

H: I just wanted to visit and see how you are.

P: That's . . .

O: Yes. It's been a while . . .

H: Maybe you're busy with more important things.

O: Oh, no, it's . . .

P: Yes, why don't you come in for a while, now that you're . . .

H: May I? Are you sure?

P: Yes, it's . . .

O: Since you're here.

H: Do you want me to take my shoes off?

P: No, that's not necessary.

H: Are you sure?

O: Since it isn't raining. I guess it's dry outside, even though it rained before.

H: I'm happy not to take my shoes off. My socks are dirty.

O: Really.

H: I have no place to wash them.

P: Aha. (SILENCE) How's Monica?

H: Well . . . I hope she's fine. She's young and strong.

O: Did something happen?

H: Yes, I guess you could say that, really, that something has happened.

P: What?

O: What happened?

H: Well, it's over.

P: What?

H: She says she is going to court tomorrow and start divorce proceedings, from me.

O: What are you saying?

H: She's starting divorce proceedings, from me.

O: Aha.

H: Yes, that's a fact. Still, it's very hard to talk about.

P: You're going to have a baby. Soon.

H: Yes, I know. I'm very aware of that.

P: But how then could . . .

H: I know. I've seen a picture of her. Of the fetus, inside the tummy. It's a girl.

O: Oh, my God, what . . .

H: Monika thinks she looks like me. She has my arms and legs, she says. . . . But I guess that's not enough.

O: What are you going to do?

H: Yes, what's there to do? I don't know. I've no idea. Not in the least. She wants it. I can't make her change her mind. There's nothing I can do. And now I've no place to live either. That's why I thought I would ask you if I could possibly stay here for a few days, while I get things together. Otherwise I'll have to find a bed in a shelter somewhere.

P: Yes, but . . .

H: I won't be a problem for you. I won't show up here very much. Now I'm getting help. I have a nice psychologist that I'm seeing once a week, and that's very positive. (SHORT PAUSE) Just for a few days, a few nights . . .

DARKNESS.
LIGHT.

14.

Q: May I come in?

X: Sure.

Q: Thank you . . . I didn't know if you were home.

X: I'm always home.

Q: How are you?

X: Where else would I be? (SILENCE)

Q: Where is he? Is he in there?

X: Yes.

Q: Yes, you sounded so . . .

X: What?

Q: . . . so tired and . . . sad. My hands are cold. I couldn't get the heat going in the car. (SHORT PAUSE) Should we go inside and see how he is?

X: Yes. (SHORT PAUSE)

Q: Come. . . . How's it going?

X: Wait.

Q: What?

X: No, I'm . . . my whole body is shaking.

Q: It is?

X: Yes.

Q: Why?

X: (QUIETLY) I don't know.

Q: So stop it.

X: Yes.

Q: Nice dress.

X: Stop it.

Q: Yea, yea, yea. So, I can't say that?

X: No.

Q: No . . . I shopped for food and wine. . . . We have to celebrate that he finally is home with you again, and that everything is going to be OK eventually . . . even though it'll take some time. (THEY WALK IN. Y IS SITTING IN THE WHEEL CHAIR. THE SUN IS SHINING. HIS EYES ARE SHUT.) Hello. . . . How are you? Is he asleep?

X: I'll turn him around.

Q: Are you sitting here enjoying yourself? (WALKS OVER TO Y, PUTS A HAND ON HIS SHOULDER.) It's me. (SHORT PAUSE) How are you? (Y LIFTS HIS HEAD AND LOOKS AT Q.) Isn't it nice to be home? Much better than being at that place, where you were, with all those . . . (PAUSE) How's it going? Any progress? (SILENCE) Has he made any progress?

X: Well, we do what we can.

Q: It won't be long now before you're playing again, just as well as you did before. The sooner you're back to normal, the better it'll be. (SHORT PAUSE) You just have to imagine it. See the picture in your mind of how you're sitting there playing.

Y: (IS TRYING TO SAY SOMETHING. THEN TRIES AGAIN.)

Q: What did he say? Did you understand what he said?

X: He'll never play again.

Q: What are you talking about? Of course he will. As good as he was . . . He's been playing since he was six years old.

Y: (TRIES TO SAY SOMETHING.) (SHORT PAUSE)

Q: You just can't give up. He can't give up.

X: He can't even lift his arms.

Q: No, but it'll come back. Wipe that thing off . . . on his face.

X: (WIPES AWAY THE DROOL FROM Y'S CHIN.) Sorry. (SHORT PAUSE) I'm just going to wipe your . . . There.

Q: So. There. (SHORT PAUSE) The room looks good after we painted it. A lot brighter. (STANDS BEHIND HER.) What do you say, should we start fixing the food? I bought three steaks from my butcher that I thought we would eat tonight. Celebrate a little. (PUTS HIS HANDS ON HER SHOULDERS.) Will he be able to eat steak if we cut it into small pieces?

X: No, only liquids.

Q: I see. Well, it's not liquid. (SILENCE)

X: Do you want something?

Y: (MAKES A SOUND.)

Q: What does he want? (Y SHAKES HIS HEAD VIOLENTLY.)

X: What are you saying?

Q: Is he saying something?

Y: Yeees, ee . . .

X: Yes? (SILENCE) What do you want to say?

Y: I e . . .

Q: I e . . .

X: What are you?

Y: I e . . . Wha e!

X: Wha e? Wha e? (SHORT PAUSE) I don't know.

Y: Eeeeee!

X: Please.... Show us.... Show us what you mean.

Y: E. (SHORT PAUSE) E.

X: E. (PAUSE) Yes.

Y: A. A. A!

X: What?

Q: Come on . . . I guess he'll soon calm down. (SHORT PAUSE) We'll have to be patient.

DARKNESS.
LIGHT.

15.

V: Anna? (SHORT PAUSE) Can you hear me? (SILENCE) Dear little Anna? (TAKES HER HAND, WHICH IS LIFELESS.) (SILENCE) Do you hear me? (SHORT PAUSE) Squeeze my hand, if you . . . (SHORT PAUSE) It's me. Daddy. I'm here. I'm here with you. (SHORT PAUSE) I'm here now. (SILENCE) They told me to hold your hand. . . . I'm supposed to hold your hand. (SHORT PAUSE) I'm holding your hand. (SHORT PAUSE) No. (SILENCE) It's snowing outside. It's been snowing for days. The trains aren't running. They stopped working because of the cold. It's so quiet. Rather pleasant, really. (SHORT PAUSE) But you must've been awfully cold. . . . I hope that you . . .

U: (ENTERS.) What are you doing here?

V: I . . .

U: What the hell are you doing here?

V: I'm just sitting here. She's asleep.

U: Why the fuck are you here?

V: What do you mean? (LOOKS AT HER.)

U: Yes, you can stare at me . . . all you want.

V: Take it easy.

U: Just think if she wakes up and you're the first one she sees. It's your fucking fault she's here in the first place.

V: (QUIETLY) Yea, yea.

U: If she dies, you're the one who killed her.

V: Sure.

U: You're killing her. She's one big, fucking wound longing to get away from her pain.

V: Yes, I don't want to . . . I don't want to talk to you.

U: Who the hell do you think want to talk to you?

V: You aren't sober. You're drunk.

U: Go to hell. If I take a drink now and then it is because I'm trying to forget the fucking hell you left us in.

V: OK, good, but could you try not to be so loud.

U: You've killed everyone around you. Soon there's nothing left.

V: (QUIETLY) I don't understand how you could come here drunk.

U: I'm the one who has the right to be here. Not you. I've cared for her since we were little. Every fucking day and night I tried to protect her and tried to get her away from your fucking mass grave.

V: Sorry?

U: No, too late to be sorry, no forgiveness, not for you.

DARKNESS.
LIGHT.

16.

G: Well, excuse me. . . . I thought I'd say hello. You're supposed to welcome the new ones. That's the least one can do.

S: Yes, yes, yes.

G: Hello, Oscar. You look the same.

S: Yes, I guess I do.

G: Do you remember me, Oscar? We were members of the building committee for many years . . . but it was long ago. Not that it is something to remember, really. Sorry, but I can't shake your hand. (SHOWS OSCAR HIS HAND.) I have pieces of glass in my hands, and it hurts like hell if I touch something. It doesn't go away. It's always there. I've had it for several years. There's nothing that can be done. I have to live with it. I don't know why I have it . . . but I can lift my hand and say hello.

DARKNESS.
LIGHT.

17.

R: What's going on?

YOUNG GIRL'S VOICE: It's me.

R: Who? . . . Go home.

YOUNG GIRL'S VOICE: I am home.

R: No one is allowed here.

YOUNG GIRL'S VOICE: (SILENCE) Your hands are so dry.

R: No, it . . .

YOUNG GIRL'S VOICE: When did you get so old? (SILENCE) Are you going to die? (SILENCE) Yes, you're going to die. That's it. You look like a mummy. (SHORT PAUSE)

R: (WHISPERS) Help me.

YOUNG GIRL'S VOICE: How?

R: Home. To go home.

YOUNG GIRL'S VOICE: Where do you live?

R: I don't know.

YOUNG GIRL'S VOICE: You don't know?

R: No.

YOUNG GIRL'S VOICE: Is it far away?

R: No, it's . . . My clothes. I have to find my clothes. Look for them.

YOUNG GIRL'S VOICE: What do they look like?

R: I don't know . . . the usual. Shoes . . . I've got to have shoes. (SILENCE) No. Wait. Don't go.

YOUNG GIRL'S VOICE: I have to.

R: No.

DARKNESS.
LIGHT.

18.

V: Anna? (SILENCE) Are you there? (SHORT PAUSE) Can you hear me? (SHORT PAUSE) Do you hear what I'm saying? (SILENCE)

Anna? Outside it's winter. It's snowing. I'm sure it's ten below. (SILENCE) Last night it was twenty below.
(SILENCE) Yes, I know.
(SHORT PAUSE) It's me. Daddy. I'm here. (SHORT PAUSE) I'm here with you. Now I'm here. I'll stay with you until you . . . (SILENCE) (U COMES IN. V NODS AT HER. U SITS DOWN.) She's asleep . . .

U: I know. (SHORT PAUSE) That's what she's doing . . .

V: Good that she's sleeping.

(THEY SIT QUIETLY FOR A WHILE.)

DARKNESS.
LIGHT.

19.

I: Well. Now we're home. (SILENCE)

J: Yes.

I: Wait, let me help you.

J: It's OK.

I: Let me help you.

J: I can take it off myself.

I: Yes, I know.

J: What did you say?

I: What did I say?

J: I don't know. That's why I asked.

I: No, I don't know either.

J: No. (SILENCE)

I: Today is the last day of April.

J: Yes, I know. . . . (SILENCE) You've been cleaning up here.

I: Yes, I did. As well as I could.

J: Yes, I can see that. (SILENCE)

I: So, how does it feel?

J: What?

I: To be home?

J: How it feels?

I: Yes.

J: I don't know how I feel. I don't feel anything.

I: Yes, but it . . .

J: How do you want me to feel? (SILENCE)

I: I bought a lobster.

J: Aha.

I: For tonight. From Canada.

J: Yes, I guess those are cheaper.

I: Yes, it was $21. That's not much.

J: No, that's cheap.

I: Yes. (PAUSE)

J: You don't have to watch me the whole time.

I: No, but . . . I'm happy to see you.

J: You are?

I: Yes I am. (SILENCE) Do you want to go out and look at the bonfire later?

J: No.

I: Around nine o'clock.

J: You go. Why don't you go?

I: I don't want to go without you. (SILENCE) Everyone will be there as usual. The condo association invited everyone to a bowl of chili.

J: Sounds delicious.

I: Everyone will ask where you are, why you aren't there . . . since everyone knows you were coming home today.

DARKNESS.
LIGHT.

20.

(WE HEAR THE SECOND PART OF SCHUBERT'S STRING QUARTET. X IS, WITH GREAT EFFORT, REMOVING Y'S SHIRT. THEN SHE PUTS SKIN CREAM ON HIS ARMS. THEN X IS TRYING TO GET Y TO LIFT HIS ARMS. BOTH OF THEM ARE TRYING TO WORK ON THE MUSCLES IN Y'S ARMS, BUT IT IS OBVIOUS THAT HE DOESN'T WANT TO, EVEN THOUGH HE IS TRYING TO LIFT HIS ARMS A FEW INCHES.)

X: Once more.

Y: Eeee . . .

X: Just one more time. Try. This is the last one.

Y: Yeees . . .

X: Yes, you can. You're doing much better. Much better than last week.

Y: Takeaeeee.

X: Yes, I'm taking your hands . . . let me stretch them backwards. (Y SHAKES HIS HEAD. IS THROWING HIS BODY BACK AND FORTH.) Stop it. Stop it.

Y: Iiiidonwanto! Iiiiidonwanto!

X: You don't want to?

Y: (THROWS HIMSELF OUT OF HER GRIP.) Nooooo! (THROWS HIMSELF FORWARD AND HITS HER WITH HIS BODY. SHE ALMOST FALLS BACKWARD.)

X: (SITS DOWN.) I don't want to either.

Y: Eeeeee! EEEEEEE!

DARKNESS.
LIGHT.

21.

C: We've seen each other almost every morning. Right here.

D: Yes.

C: For half a year.

D: Really.

C: Even longer. Since March. (SHORT PAUSE) I've seen you anyway. (PAUSE) Sometimes there's been a man coming here, after you've sat down.

D: My husband.

C: Yes, I thought so . . . and a little boy.

D: Yes, our son.

C: But most of the time you've been sitting here all alone when I've been coming in with my computer. . . . (SILENCE) I was surprised when you said hello this morning, when you suddenly said hello.

D: Yes, I . . .

C: It made me happy. And . . . (PAUSE) I didn't really dare to do it myself, even though I had . . . tried. . . . That's why I . . .

D: Yes.

C: . . . when I saw that you didn't take out your computer. (PAUSE) But I haven't seen you for some time.

D: No, I haven't been here.

C: Not for several months. I thought you might have moved . . .

D: No. (SHORT PAUSE)

C: It's snowing again.

D: Yes. He's dead.

C: Who?

D: He died. My husband. Henrik.

C: Henrik?

D: Yes.

C: He's dead?

D: Yes, he died.

C: The one I saw, the one who was with you when I saw you?

D: Yes, Henrik.

C: Really. (PAUSE)

D: I don't know how long ago. The sixteenth. Monday the sixteenth. Almost two months. (SHORT PAUSE) Today is the first time I've gone out. Out of the house. Except for the funeral.

C: Yes.

D: But I don't know what I'm doing here. Why I'm sitting here . . . drinking coffee.

C: No.

D: I don't know what I'm doing here. What I'm going to do.

C: No, I know. That's what . . . what I noticed. (SHORT PAUSE) That's why I . . . (PAUSE)

D: I feel like I haven't talked to anyone for many years.

C: No.

D: Just with Johan.

C: Your son?

D: Yes. Johan.

C: Yes.

D: He's talking now. He talks all day long. He asks the same question. (SILENCE) He stands by the window and says: Daddy is coming soon? Daddy is coming? (SHORT PAUSE) But he isn't.

C: How did he die? Can you tell me?

D: Yes.

C: Was he ill?

D: He took his own life.

C: I see. Well . . . (D SHAKES HER HEAD FOR A LONG TIME.) No. (PAUSE)

D: He threw himself in front of a train in the subway. He was supposed to come home the usual time, around seven thirty. But he never came home.

DARKNESS.
LIGHT.

22.

E: Where are you? (SHORT PAUSE) I see. (SILENCE) Is everything OK? (SHORT PAUSE) Is everyone having fun? (SHORT PAUSE) Yes. (SILENCE) No, I'm here. I'm at home. Where else would I be? (SILENCE) When will you be home? (SHORT PAUSE) No. (SILENCE) She's awake. (SHORT PAUSE) She's sitting next to me. Do you want to talk to her? Do you want to talk to Daddy? (SILENCE) Yes, say something to Daddy.

Ee: Hello. Watched TV. (SILENCE) No. I already read it. (SHORT PAUSE) I've already read it. (SILENCE) Yes. Good night. Bye, then.

E: Don't hang up.

Ee: Yes. I love you too. Bye, bye.

E: (TAKES THE PHONE.) It's me. (SILENCE) Yes. (SILENCE) Are you at Veronika's? (SILENCE) Yes, I know . . . I know everything.

DARKNESS.
LIGHT.

23.

Q: I'm sorry. I couldn't see. (SHORT PAUSE)

R: Yes.

Q: I noticed that the light in the elevator is out. How are you?

R: Fine . . .

Q: Is there anything . . . Do you want me to help you?

R: No. No one can.

Q: I can take your paper bag.

R: It's mine.

Q: So you won't drop it.

R: I'm going there.

Q: I understand. That's where you're going.

R: There's no name on the door. Only my name.

Q: Yes, I . . .

R: I used to live there.

Q: So you're not living there now?

R: I used to.

Q: OK . . . Are you sure you'll be OK?

DARKNESS.
LIGHT.

24.

O: What are you doing?

H: I'm just sitting here.

O: I see, yes . . .

H: Is it OK?

O: Yes, sure.

H: That I'm sitting here.

O: Of course.

H: Thank you. (SILENCE) I'm really grateful that I can stay here for a couple of days, here with you, in your warm embrace, I really am. But it feels a little strange to be sitting in that little room for days on end. It was easier back then, being a boy and all. At that time one had all kinds of interests, but now it isn't . . . Also, one was smaller then, physically I mean.

O: Yes, it . . .

H: But I'm really grateful that I've got someplace to stay for now.

O: Yes. (SHORT PAUSE)

H: What's wrong?

O: Sorry?

H: What are you looking at?

O: Looking?

H: Yes, you're looking at me. Do I look strange?

O: Strange? No . . . no, you don't. Not that I can see.

H: Where's Mom?

O: Where she is? She was going to the optician to pick up my new glasses.

H: Are your eyes bad?

O: Yes, obviously my eyes are getting worse.

H: But you do see me? Sitting here?

O: Yes, you aren't sitting that far away. I have a cataract in my right eye.

H: The right one?

O: Yes, the left one is OK for now. (SILENCE) Maybe you should go out a little?

H: Go out?

O: Get some air.

H: Out?

O: Wouldn't it be nice to go out and get a little fresh air?

H: It was long ago that the air was fresh. Yes, if people only wouldn't stare at me the whole time.

O: Stare?

H: Yes. At me.

O: Really.

H: Maybe it's just in my imagination. Do you think so?

O: Yes, that's what it sounds like.

H: But why am I imagining it now? (SILENCE) Well.

O: (SILENCE) I really . . .

H: No?

O: So . . . have you . . . have you had any contact with Monica lately?

H: No.

O: No, I see.

DARKNESS.
LIGHT.

25.

X: Come on. Come on now.

Y: Noooo.

X: Help me a little. (SHORT PAUSE) Push.

Y: Noooo.

X: I know you can. (SHORT PAUSE) Just a little longer. A little longer.

Y: Eeh, eeh, eeh, eeh, eeh!

X: You've got to push.

Y: Iiiiiidon't!

X: I know. One more time. Just once more. Please calm down. Try.

Y: Iiiiiidon't! (HE IS BARECHESTED, VERY THIN, AND IS THROWING HIMSELF BACK AND FORTH.)

X: You have to. Otherwise you'll wither away.

Y: Aaaaaaah!

X: Is that what you want?

Y: Yes! Yes! Yes! Ah! (FALLS FORWARD ONTO HER. IS HANGING ON HER. SHE DOESN'T HAVE ENOUGH STRENGTH TO CARRY HIM, SINKS DOWN, IS SITTING STILL TRYING TO GATHER HER STRENGTH, TRIES TO GET HIM TO SIT UP AGAIN.)

X: (QUIETLY) I can't take it. I can't take it any longer.

Y: Eeeeeeeeeeehh!

X: No . . . (PAUSE) I'm sorry.

Y: Noooooo. Eeeeeeee.

X: Is that what you want? That I won't be able to take it anymore? Is that what you want?

Y: Yeeeees. Aaaaaah. AH!

X: It's not my fault. I can't . . . (PAUSE) I can't leave. (SILENCE) Hey, you. (PAUSE) Look at me. (Y TURNS HIS HEAD AWAY.) Give the hell up then. Just give the hell up. (SILENCE) (FETCHES A LONG-SLEEVED, DIRTY T-SHIRT.) You're the only one who can . . . (WIPES HIS CHIN, MOUTH AND STOMACH, AND THEN PULLS THE T-SHIRT OVER HIS HEAD.) (PAUSE) What am I to do? (PICKS UP THE BOOK, *A MYSTICAL FRIENDSHIP*, OFF THE FLOOR.) Should we read for a little while? (Y PUSHES THE BOOK OUT OF HER HANDS.) That was very good. You can as long as you really want to.

Q: (COMES IN CARRYING A LOT OF TOOLS.) Hello! (SILENCE) Anybody home? (ENTERS THE ROOM.) Are you in here?

X: Yes.

Q: Good. I think I have everything I need. There are two bags of cement in the car. I think that should be enough. The electrician will be here at seven a.m. tomorrow morning. (SILENCE) I thought I'd start demolishing the old one tonight, so that I wouldn't have as much to do tomorrow, since he's coming here so early. What's wrong? (SILENCE) How's it going? (SILENCE) Is he making any progress?

X: (QUIETLY) I don't know.

Q: No, I can tell. (SHORT PAUSE) No, it's . . .

DARKNESS.
LIGHT.

ACT 2.

1.

(SNOW IS FALLING QUIETLY. A NUMBER OF PEOPLE ARE WALKING AROUND WHILE THE SNOW IS FALLING. EACH ONE OF THEM IS HOLDING A BOOK THAT THEY ARE READING OR NOT READING.)

DARKNESS.
LIGHT.

2.

F: Are you watching it again?

E: No.

F: Why do you do that? (SILENCE) You can hardly tell who it is.

E: It's a different one. Only the two of you are in it. I'm not there. I wasn't around yet. (SILENCE)

F: Where is it?

E: How would I know?

F: It must've been . . .

E: Before I existed. (SHORT PAUSE) There you are . . . and him.

F: Yes, I can see for myself.

E: You look happy.

F: Really . . . happy?

E: Can't you see that? (SILENCE) The whole you . . . you're shining.

F: I guess I was.

E: But it's hard to believe. (SILENCE) (TURNS AROUND AND LOOKS AT F.) Her . . . in the white bathing suit . . . who's she? (SILENCE) Don't you see her?

F: Yes, that's . . .

E: She's laughing hysterically.

F: That's Agnes.

E: Agnes?

F: We saw each other often those years. She was my best girlfriend.

E: (SILENCE) Anyway, he's really good looking. (SHORT PAUSE) Tall and thin and suntanned. . . . And he knows it.

F: Who?

E: You know, he, who's my dad. He was very good looking.

F: Yes, I guess that's why I fell for him.

E: What happened to her?

F: Who?

E: Agnes.

F: I don't know. . . . What happens to us?

E: What did you say?

F: I don't know what happened to her. . . . You go in different directions. (SILENCE) Sometimes.

E: Don't you want to watch anymore?

F: No. (SHORT PAUSE) I've forgotten them.

E: I want to watch. Want to see everything. Every second. I want to know how it was. (SILENCE)

F: How it was?

E: Since you never tell me anything.

F: There's nothing more to tell . . . that I remember.

E: Why he left.

F: Well, I guess he was like that. One of those who leaves.

E: I want to know whom I was longing for.

F: I don't know who he is.

E: Who didn't show up. And whom I was waiting for.

F: One day he left and never came back.

E: There I am on the swing set. (SILENCE)

F: I was only twenty-two years old.

DARKNESS.
LIGHT.

3.

O: You don't want to eat?

H: No.

O: (H PULLS AT THE TABLE CLOTH.) Really.

P: I thought it was good.

H: Why do you say "was" when you're still eating?

P: I'm not done yet.

O: This is what you liked the most when you were a little boy.

H: Not anymore, right?

O: What?

H: Little. Little.

O: No, but . . .

H: That was quite a few years ago. Little and defenseless. Playing with my Legos. (STRAIGHTENS OUT THE TABLE CLOTH.) My Lego set is probably worth something today, if one were to sell it.

O: You might be right.

H: Could we try to keep the tablecloth straight? Could it possibly stay straight along the edges of the table, instead of being pulled to the side. There's more tablecloth on the other side than on this side. Since we're sitting in a rectangle.

P: What do you mean?

O: The tablecloth?

H: Yes, you're pulling at it, so it becomes asymmetrical.

O: Really.

P: Why does it matter?

H: That's wrong. Uneven. Unsymmetrical. Unbalanced.

P: Aha . . .

H: Aren't you aware of that?

O: No, we never thought about that.

H: No, I know. (SILENCE) Now it's straight. The way it's supposed to be. Thank you. (SILENCE)

O: It's snowing again.

P: Again?

O: Yes, it never ends.

H: There's not a single thing that's been moved or added to in this room in thirty years. (SILENCE)

O: Do you want some more?

P: No thanks. No thank you.

H: It looks exactly the way it did when you were married and moved in here.

O: Yes, but we are . . . We have what we need.

P: We don't need anything else.

H: Can't you sit still?

P: What is it now?

H: Sit still. Absolutely still. Sit still.

O: What are you doing?

H: The crease.

O: The crease?

H: In the tablecloth. I can't stand creases. I can't stand it when tablecloths and sheets and towels aren't ironed and folded correctly. Like this tablecloth. It isn't smooth. The edges are wrinkled. They aren't straight. The way they are supposed to be. They are uneven. Not the way they are supposed to be. They are supposed to be even and smooth. Even and smooth. Not uneven.

P: Then don't look at it, if it makes you feel bad.

H: We might as well get rid of it—completely. There's no other way.

O: No but . . .

P: Take it easy.

H: I'm taking it easy.

P: No, it . . .

H: I'm falling apart.

P: Falling apart?

H: Yes, I am. Completely. I'm feeling the same way I do when someone is coming up behind me wearing shoes that make noises that sound like gunshots, or me being hit by a sledgehammer. I feel like killing someone.

DARKNESS.
LIGHT.

4.

X: Do you have a cell phone?

B: Everyone has a cell phone.

X: I thought if something happened.

B: It's an old one.

X: But it's working, isn't it?

B: They said you'd give me a credit card if you needed something.

X: Yes, I'm giving you cash. (WIPES Y'S MOUTH.) This is Nike. (Y SHAKES HIS HEAD.)

B: Hello.

X: He can't say that many words yet.

B: No, no.

X: No words, really.

B: OK.

X: Well . . . then . . . (SILENCE) This is the first time he has a personal assistant. I told him you were coming, and that the two of you were going out for a little while, alone, just you two.

B: Yes.

X: So we'll see how it works out. This is really just a test . . . to see how you two . . .

B: Yes. (SILENCE) How long should we be gone?

X: What do you think? A couple of hours, maybe?

B: I didn't dress very warmly, because I didn't know if I were supposed to stay at home with him.

X
No, it . . . but maybe you could go for a little walk . . . maybe to Bloom's café down there, if it's too cold. There they have room for a wheel chair anyway, and he was there before with me, both before and after . . . Did I give you the key?

B: Yes.

X: OK. (WIPES Y'S MOUTH.) If you want to, you could go down to the museum and listen to some music or check out if there's some interesting show happening, . . . but I don't think he'd like to do that.

B: No.

X: Just as long as he gets out a little.

B: OK.

DARKNESS.
LIGHT.

5.

I: Is she kicking?

J: I don't know. (PAUSE)

I: Now she kicked.

J: I know.

I: I could see it.

J: I felt it.

I: Yes, that's a hell of a difference. (PAUSE) Let me feel your tummy? (PUTS HIS HAND ON HER STOMACH.) No.

J: No.

I: What?

J: As soon as you touch me she stops.

I: Really. (SHORT PAUSE)

J: I guess she doesn't want to perform. (SILENCE)

I: What's wrong?

J: What? (SILENCE)

I: Say something.

J: Say something?

I: Yes.

J: What's there to say?

I: I don't know.

J: Me neither.

I: No.

J: No. (PAUSE)

I: What do you think I should have done? (SILENCE) Were you hoping that I had started to fight with them? That I should've kicked them in the heads until they dropped. (SHORT PAUSE) I called the police.

J: That was good.

I: Yes.

J: They weren't much better when they came.

I: It wasn't my fault . . .

J: That's not what this is about.

I: So, what is it about then?

J: What would you've done if they had attacked me instead?

I: What do you think?

J: I really don't know.

I: I really don't know? What do you mean by that? (SILENCE)

J: I don't know. (SHORT PAUSE) Was it because he wasn't American that everyone just stood there and watched while they almost killed him?

I: There was no time. It happened so quickly.

J: Everyone just stood and watched.

I: You too.

J: What the hell, I'm pregnant. I'm in my seventh month, with your child.

I: Yes, I know.

J: I don't want her to grow up in this kind of world.

I: I see.

J: Where ordinary people just stand and watch while a human being is almost killed without anyone reacting.

I: I reacted. I did what I could.

J: I don't know if I want to live in a world like that. I can't live in this world . . . with my child.

I: So, what kind of world can you live in then?

DARKNESS.
LIGHT.

6.

C: What can I get you?

D: I have to leave before three.

C: Sure, but . . .

D: I told them I'd pick him up at three-thirty today.

C: Is it a good day care?

D: You have to write down the time when you pick them up, so that they know who's there or not . . . if something were to happen.

C: Yes.

D: Before I didn't think anything could happen, but now I know that . . .

C: Yes. Is it a good day care?

D: Yes, I think so. Today they were going to the Aquarium in the morning.

C: What fun.

D: To check out sea creatures and turtles.

C: That's right. I was there with Sanna. Patting the Boa Constrictor, who, at that time, was fifteen years old. She didn't dare to pat him. What a life, to lie there and be patted for fifteen years.

D: Yesterday we cleaned the schoolyard. All the parents, no, not all of them, but many of them. (SILENCE)

C: Sorry.

D: Yes . . .

C: I can feel how long it's been since I touched someone.

D: Yes. (C TAKES HER LEFT HAND.) What time is it?

C: I don't know. (SHORT PAUSE) Come.

D: Yes. What?

C: Come . . . (IS KISSING HER.) (SILENCE) What's wrong? (SILENCE) You aren't really here.

D: No. (SILENCE) Why am I here?

C: Because . . .

D: No.

C: I don't know. (SILENCE)

D: My world is so small.

C: Small?

D: There's a boy who's three years old and who's beginning to understand that his Dad isn't coming home to him anymore, and a man that I love who's dead . . . who I thought was happy with me and with what we had.

C: Yes, but . . . maybe he was. Maybe it was just a mistake. (SILENCE) What are you looking at?

D: Over there?

C: Yes. What? (SHORT PAUSE) The picture?

D: The woman.

C: Yes.

D: Do you know her?

C: The one in the picture?

D: Yes.

C: Well . . . otherwise I guess I wouldn't . . .

D: How?

C: Well, how . . .

D: Yes, how do you know . . .

C: That's my wife.

D: Emilia?

C: Yes. Do you know her?

D: Yes.

C: You do?

D: Yes, of course I do.

C: How?

D: I've known her since we were in college. We were in the same class. We were best friends. We were always together, for many years. She always helped me. She protected me . . . against all evil.

C: Emma?

D: The last time I saw her we were chained together in a police vehicle, because we had been arrested for demonstrating against Bush.

(SILENCE)

C: Are you . . . is your name Veronika?

D: I really liked her.

C: Yes. Me too.

D: Very much. I've missed her.

C: She, well . . .

D: I've missed her very much.

C: Yes, but . . . but that was long ago.

D: Nothing is long ago. (SILENCE) She looks exactly as I remember her, full of expectation and very happy . . . Anything could make her happy.

C: Yes, there she was . . .

D: I've got to go.

C: No.

DARKNESS.
LIGHT.

7.

K: Is that you?

L: Isn't that what we said?

K: We did?

L: Yes.

K: Really . . . (SHORT PAUSE)

L: Is she sleeping?

K: Hope so. . . . (SILENCE) Well?

L: I just wanted to talk about her schedule.

K: Her schedule? What fucking schedule?

L: When she's supposed to be with me.

K: We've already talked about that.

L: Yes, I know, but . . .

K: Are you changing everything again?

L: No.

K: You've never kept to anything we've decided anyway.

L: No, but . . .

K: Am I right?

L: I've been sick.

K: You've been sick?

L: Yes, that's what I said.

K: You haven't seen her for two weeks.

L: You didn't let me see her the weekend before.

K: That only happened once.

L: Once?

K: Yes, one fucking time.

L: Really.

K: Yes. Isn't that right?

L: Well, then that's it. Monday, Wednesday and Thursday.

K: What do you want to change?

L: No, nothing.

K: No? (PAUSE)

L: Can I pick her up tomorrow?

K: No.

L: Tomorrow is Wednesday.

K: Yes, I know.

L: Why can't I?

K: It won't work.

L: What about Thursday?

K: Yes. That might be possible . . . (SILENCE) What is it?

L: I just wanted to see if I'm still here.

K: Still here? You're standing here.

L: The pictures . . . of me. If they are still here.

K: I took them away. Except for one. So that she can show other . . .

L: Show whom?

K: Other people.

L: Who is she going to show the pictures to?

K: Anyone. (SILENCE)

L: I thought we might buy a new baby stroller.

K: Well, then, you do it. I've no money.

L: I want to be able to look at her.

K: Right now she wants to see what's coming towards her.

L: Sure. (SHORT PAUSE) The most important thing is to talk to her.

K: Don't you think I talk to her?

L: Sure I do.

K: Talk to her? I talk to her the whole time, from morning to evening and almost every night. All I do is talk to her.

DARKNESS.
LIGHT.

8.

R: Who is it?

W: It's me. (SILENCE)

R: I'm sick. (SHORT PAUSE) I'm not at home.

W: No, I know.

R: I'm someplace else.

W: Don't you recognize me? (SILENCE)

R: I don't know.

W: Don't you see who I am?

R: No.

W: Can I come in?

R: No. I'm sick. I don't feel well. Why don't you come another day?

W: No. (SILENCE)

R: What do you want?

W: I just wanted to see how you are.

R: I'm in bad shape.

W: Yes, you told me.

R: Yes. (SILENCE) I don't have the time.

W: For what?

R: I've done what I was supposed to do. (SILENCE) Now you can't say anything anyway. I've the right to do what I want to do.

W: I'm not saying anything.

R: With the time I've left.

W: That's fine. (REMAINS WHERE HE IS STANDING.) I guess there isn't much time left.

R: That's my right. To live the way I want to, and to die the way I want to.

W: Sure.

R: I've already died once. I didn't get any help then. No one came. I was alone until she came and helped me. Next time I'll die for real.

W: Who came?

R: The girl.

W: What girl?

R: I don't know her name. (SHORT PAUSE)

W: I'm here only because Dad asked me to look for you. A friend of Dad's saw you outside a liqueur store begging for money. You were only wearing slippers and the temperature was ten below. And you'd wet your pants, too. He asked me to go and see if you were still alive.

R: Who?

W: Dad.

R: Who's that?

W: Dad. Bertil, The one you were married to for fifteen years.

R: Yes . . . I don't remember. (SILENCE) Do you have any money . . . to give to me?

W: No.

R: Since I'm your mother.

DARKNESS.
LIGHT.

9.

T: Tell me.

U: Yes. (PAUSE) I can't. (SILENCE)

T: Try.

U: Yes.

T: Well?

U: I'm cold. (SILENCE)

T: What are you thinking about right now?

U: Right now?

T: Yes.

U: Well, I'm thinking . . .

T: Yes?

U: About that. (SILENCE)

T: About that?

U: Yes. Her.

T: Who?

U: Mommy.

T: Yes. (SILENCE)

U: She didn't feel very well.

T: No. (SILENCE) That seems obvious.

U: My Dad leaves her. Leaves us. I was a little girl. My sister was even younger. Two years younger than me. I kind of take care of her, kind of protect her, as well as I can . . . against her, against mommy when she doesn't feel so well . . . as well as she should, I mean. But that's not all the time, but then we don't get enough food and stuff. Sometimes she's very strange. You can't like reach her. But sometimes she is happy, almost too happy, laughing and singing and carrying on, mostly laughing at her own jokes, and we try to laugh with her. Sometimes she isn't there at all. Just sits there staring. In the beginning she was just depressed, but then it got worse and worse. Maybe she's trying her best, I don't know. Sometimes it could be good for many days in a row, really very good. We had good days, too, ordinary days, but not that many, but I try to remember those days, when she was feeling happy. When she washed herself and combed her hair and got dressed like a normal mother . . . but that was only . . . not that often. I think the worst part was her silence and that you didn't know what was going to happen, how she was feeling . . . if it was going to be good or terrible.

(SILENCE)

T: Yes.

U: Yes. That time she said that we were going to take a bath, both of us. We usually didn't do that because our tub was so small, not big enough for both of us. I think I was about seven then, maybe eight. No older than eight. She said that we were taking a bath in the tub. I had already filled it with water. Hurry up and get undressed, she said. Her voice was sweet. Almost warm. I remember testing the water carefully, because I didn't know if the water would be too hot, but it wasn't. She had bought bubble bath stuff too. Anna liked that. Bubble bath for kids. There were a lot of bubbles. Jump in, she said. So we did. We always did everything she said, so that she wouldn't be sad. (PAUSE)

T: And then? (PAUSE) What happened then?

U: Then. Well, we went into the tub and sat there. Then she turned the light off and then she pushed me and Anna down under the water. She pushed us hard. Under the water. I remember that I was fighting for my life and I saw her face, but I don't know how long I was fighting. But suddenly she wasn't holding me down any longer and I managed to get out of the tub and then I got Anna out . . . (SHORT PAUSE) Then she was sitting on the floor crying. . . . (SILENCE) Are you there?

T: Yes, I'm here.

U: You didn't fall asleep, did you?

T: No. (SILENCE)

U: I used to go to someone who fell asleep . . . I turned around and I saw him sleeping.

T: I don't fall asleep.

U: Well . . . (SILENCE) yes, that was that. (SILENCE)

T: Tell it to me again. (SHORT PAUSE) Tell me once more.

DARKNESS.
LIGHT.

10.

G: They were heading a Christian mission in China. That was in the thirties. At that time it took a long time to go to China, but that's where they had decided that they were going, the further away the better. They had four children that they left behind in order to take care of some poor unchristian Chinese children. He lived to be ninety-three years old, but toward the end of his life he became senile . . . and then everything that he'd suppressed came out: his belief in God, his discipline and his clean living. Everything broke down . . . and he became a terror, someone without any boundaries . . .

S: Do you have to be so loud?

G: I'm sorry. (STANDS UP.) Am I talking too loudly?

S: One can't even think.

DARKNESS.
LIGHT.

11.

(THE ROOM IS FILLED WITH ALL THE PEOPLE WHO HAVE ALREADY APPEARED IN THE PLAY. A WOMAN PASSES BY.)

C: Are you hungry?

Ee: No.

C: You're never hungry. (SILENCE) You aren't eating enough.

Ee: I think I do. (SILENCE) Why are they so quiet?

C: I don't know. Maybe they don't know what to say.

Ee: What are they waiting for?

C: Yes, what are they waiting for? (SILENCE)

Ee: Well . . .

C: Let's walk home . . . then we'll have a little more time together. (SILENCE) Do you remember that we used to come here and play on the swings after I had picked you up from daycare when you were little?

Ee: Yes.

C: It didn't matter what kind of weather it was . . . until you got tired.

Ee: Yes. . . . Was Mommy dead then?

C: What are you saying? Which Mommy?

Ee: I don't . . .

C: Why do you say things like that? (SHORT PAUSE) What were you thinking of?

Ee: I don't know. Nothing. (SILENCE)

C: You can't say things like that. Or . . . I guess you can. . . . I'll pick you up tomorrow.

Ee: Yes. . . . What are we going to do?

C: Whatever you want to do. (SILENCE) What do you want to do?

Ee: I don't know.

C: Are you tired?

Ee: No, are you?

C: No. (SILENCE) I love you.

Ee: I know.

C: Good. (SILENCE) Let's go.

eE: Yes. (SHORT PAUSE) Where?

C: Home.

Ee: To you?

C: No, to you.

Ee: To you and me.

C: No, to you. . . . I'll carry your bag.

DARKNESS.

12.

W: Have you been waiting long?

U: Long, yes. (SILENCE) Yes, I've been waiting a long time.

W: That's why there are so many people here.

U: What do you mean by that?

W: People waiting.

U: Yes.

W: Well . . . where are you going?

U: Home, probably.

W: Really.

U: Yes.

W: What's your name?

U: Sorry?

W: I asked what your name is.

U: Rakel.

W: Rakel?

U: Yes.

W: I have no name.

U: You've been sitting here for a long time.

W: Yes, I'm in no hurry.

U: You were already here when I came. I thought I saw you.

W: Yes. (SILENCE) I can't accept the word "self murderer." If I take my own life I'm not a murderer. I don't murder myself. I just end my life. I'm letting it happen. I liberate myself mercifully from myself. It's a simple liberation. I decide that I don't want to live. Nothing more than that. Look at any pro-suicide site and you'll see. We can look together if you want.

DARKNESS.
LIGHT.

13.

Q: I'm sorry. (SILENCE) I just wanted to see you. (SILENCE) (TAKES HER HAND, CARESSES IT AS IF IT WAS A VISION, THE ONLY HAND IN THE WORLD.)

X: (HER HAND LIFELESS, ALLOWS HIM TO CARESS IT. HE TRIES TO OPEN IT, AS IF HE WANTED TO PUT SOMETHING IN IT.) (SHORT PAUSE) Didn't we decide that you weren't supposed to come here again?

Q: I know . . . I know what we said.

X: Only when he's at home.

Q: But what am I to do?

X: You can't come here. It has to end. I get . . .

Q: When will he be back?

X: Any moment. He could be here any moment now. (SILENCE)

Q: Does she seem good, his personal assistant?

X: I don't know. He hasn't said anything, anyway. (SILENCE) I know what he sees . . . when he sees you. (SILENCE) I can feel it.

Q: Look at me. Now.

X: No . . .

Q: Yes. (PAUSE) Do you want me to leave? (PAUSE) Do you? Is that what you want?

X: You have to see him. He's your son.

Q: I can't live without you.

X: But you are, aren't you? (SHORT PAUSE) (Q PICKS UP THE BOOK FROM THE TABLE.)

Q: Look. (DROPS THE BOOK. IT FALLS ON THE FLOOR.) What just happened?

X: The book fell on the floor.

Q: Yes it did. It's just as hard for me to stop loving you as it is for the book not to fall on the floor if it's dropped. (REACHES OUT TO TOUCH HER HAIR.)

X: You are not a book.

Q: No, but that's how I feel.

X: (BENDS HER HEAD DOWN.) No.

Q: Look at me. (SHORT PAUSE)

X: No . . . no.

Q: You're afraid . . . you're afraid to show your face . . . because then I'll see how much you like me. . . . I'll see that you feel the same way . . . if I see your face.

X: I'll die . . . I'll die from this . . . from what I've done. I'll be punished.

DARKNESS.
LIGHT.

14.

B: Jello?

Y: Nooo. Sch, Schsccch . . . ello.

B: Ello?

Y: Nooo. Ssch, sccch, scheelooo.

B: Tjelo.

Y: Umumum.

B: I gave you ice cream.

Y: Mu mumu . . .

B: Mu, yes.

Y: Muss muss . . . iiiic.

B: Music?

Y: Ah, ahahah.

B: Sure. Sure.

Y: Ah!

B: You want to listen to music? Do you have an iphone?

Y: Iiisaid . . . Iiiisaid . . . Iiiisaid.

B: Yes, that's what I said. (SILENCE)

Y: (CALMLY AND SLOWLY) Iiisaid. Yes.

B: OK. (Y'S BODY FALLS FORWARD. AGAIN HE FALLS FORWARD.) Stop it. Sit still. (LIFTS HIM BACK. HE FALLS FORWARD AGAIN.) What the hell, stop it! Why won't you sit up straight? (Y IS MOVING BACK AND FORTH WHILE B IS LIFTING HIM. HE LOOKS HAPPY.) Your whole face is full of spit. (Y FALLS FORWARD AGAIN.) Now I'm leaving you like that. Do you hear me?

Y: Iiiisaid!

B: Yes, I hear you . . .

Y: Ican. Ican. Ican. . . .

B: What the hell are they looking at? (WIPES Y'S FACE WITH A WET TISSUE.)

Y: Ican. Ican. Ican.

B: That son of a bitch has been staring at us for half an hour, and now he pretends that he is not. Now he's looking at the hot dog stand instead, fucking asshole.

DARKNESS.
LIGHT.

15.

A DARK ROOM.

H: (SHORT PAUSE) Let's be quiet. Let's be quiet!

O: We are, aren't we?

P: Why don't we turn on the TV.

O: Yes, why don't we.

P: It's almost seven. The news will be on.

O: Yes.

H: There's nothing new. Nothing that makes you feel good anyway.

O: I like to know what's happening.

H: Nothing new is happening.

O: You don't know that.

H: I can tell you everything.

O: We usually look at the TV news, every night.

H: The light is too bright.

P: Too bright?

H: After a while you turn into a rabbit.

(SILENCE)

P: What did he say?

O: Rabbit.

P: Rabbit?

H: You turn into a rabbit. Who's sitting there shaking of fear. In the floodlight.

(SILENCE)

P: (QUIETLY) What are you going to do?

H: Just sit. Soon you two are going to bed. You're tired. You're old. You shouldn't stay up and watch shit.

O: I'm not going to bed.

P: This early?

H: Let's just sit here. Calmly and quietly. In silence. Let's not talk. Let's not move around. We'll be quiet. Our breathing will be calm. We'll be thinking beautiful thoughts. Memories. Nice memories. Family outings. Days filled with sunshine. We are bicycling. We're going to the lake. We're going swimming. We undress. We brought a picnic basket. We put it in the shade. We sit for a while in the sunshine.

O: What is . . .

H: Quiet. Be quiet, I said.

O: I don't want to be quiet.

P: We haven't said anything.

O: No.

H: So that I don't have to listen to your suddenly remembered fucking memories of how it used to be.
O: Maybe Robert will come by soon.

P: Yes, I'm sure he will.

O: He comes by now and then, Robert. Your brother. Our son.
(SILENCE)

O: What's wrong?

P: I'm afraid.

O: Why?

H: Afraid?

P: Yes.

H: Yes, you have every reason to be afraid.

O: We do?

H: Yes.

P: Why do you talk like that?

H: I would be afraid.

O: What's going on?

P: Erik?

O: Dear Erik . . .

P: Yes.

O: Please let us leave.

H: Yes, as long as you beg me.

P: Just let us leave.

O: We'll just leave.

P: Leave here.

H: Beg me. Go down on your bare knees and beg me.

O: Beg you?

H: On your bare knees.

O: What are we begging for?

DARKNESS.
LIGHT.

16.

T: How long have you known each other?

B: Forever.

A: For quite a while.

T: Forever.

B: Yes.

T: How long is that?

A: About a year, I guess.

B: Longer.

A: Since April last year I think. That's when we met. Almost a year ago. In two months. This April.

T: I see. (PAUSE) Well, well.

B: What?

T: Nothing. (PAUSE)
B: It feels longer.

A: Yes, but it . . .

B: Longer than just a year.

A: Yes, but it isn't.

B: No, I know.

A: Yes. Sure. (PAUSE)

T: What kind of work do you do?

B: Write that I'm in health care.

T: I guess I can do that. So, I guess it isn't . . .

B: People always ask what you do, as if that should mean something, as if that's who you are.

T: Yes, that's . . .

A: Right now I'm working as a super in a building for a buddy of mine, who's managing a couple of buildings. He went away on a trip for a couple of months to relax and do some deep sea diving and drinking.

T: Aha.

A: But that's just for a couple of months. Then I'm going to take a computer course.

T: Really.

A: At the community college.

B: That's where we met.

A: Yes, that's right. I noticed her the first day she was there.

B: It feels much longer when you are together day and night the way we are. It's as if time itself is longer.

A: Yes, except when I'm working. Or you're working. Otherwise we're together all the time.
T: Yes, I'd heard that you're a personal assistant to someone. Someone told me that.

B: Yes, I know.

T: Is that right?

B: Yea. (SILENCE)

T: How's that?

B: How is it?

T: To care for someone else? Is it tough, or . . .

B: What do you think?

T: I'm sure it is.

A: May I use the bathroom?

T: Sure. (A LEAVES.) (PAUSE, QUIETLY) What happened to his body?

B: What?

T: He seems deformed. His back and his shoulder are deformed. Completely out of whack.

B: His dad kicked his mom when he was in her tummy. He kicked her in the stomach when she was pregnant.

T: I see.

B: He doesn't want to see him anymore, his real dad from birth. He doesn't want to call him Dad.

T: I see.

B: Do you have a cigarette?

T: No, sorry, I don't smoke.

DARKNESS.
LIGHT.

17.

(N, THE NURSE FROM SCENE 9, ACT 1.)

(SILENCE)

V: Yes, here we are. The two of us.

N: Yes, here we are. (PAUSE) I can't believe it.

V: Well . . . Does it feel strange? (THEY ARE SITTING ON A BED IN A MOTEL ROOM.)

N: Nothing I'm used to, anyway.

V: I'm not either.

N: It feels clean anyway.

V: (SILENCE) I've really never done anything like this before. I feel a little nervous.

N: Yes, I do too. (SHORT PAUSE) (FEELS THE BEDSPREAD WITH HER HAND.) What you see looks clean anyway.

V: Yes.

N: We aren't going to live here, are we? (SHORT PAUSE) I've never done this either. This is a new experience.

V: Yes. (SHORT PAUSE) Did you say you had to work late?

N: No. (SHORT PAUSE) I don't have to say anything. I don't say anything. We don't talk very much. These days.

V: I know.

N: We stopped talking many years ago.

V: Yes, I know about that.

N: But I can't leave him now.

V: No, I . . . I understand. I can't either. (SILENCE) Wait. I bought a bottle of champagne.

N: Champagne? Really.

V: Yes, for us. It should be cold, but . . . sorry, plastic glasses.

N: Doesn't matter.

V: I've got to be careful not to get it all over me. (OPENS THE BOTTLE, POURS CHAMPAGNE INTO THE PLASTIC GLASSES.) Please . . . dear . . .

N: Thank you.

V: Cheers. (THEY DRINK.) I have to say that I . . . that I can't tell you how incredibly happy I am that I saw you in the drugstore and that I found the courage to say hello. (SHORT PAUSE) Did you recognize me . . . in spite of . . .

N: Of course I did. Right away. Even before you noticed me . . . I saw it was you.

V: We aren't really hurting anyone. (PAUSE)

N: No . . . Aren't we?

V: It seems like we're both stuck in our . . . rather unsatisfying marriages.

N: Yes. (SILENCE) What are you doing?

V: I'm looking for . . . for . . . for . . .

N: What?

V: Well, you know . . . the rubbers. I forgot to bring them.

N: Rubbers?

V: Yes, you know. Condoms.

N: Condoms?

V: I bought a pack at the gas station when we stopped.

N: You're kidding, right? Don't you know how old I am?

V: To be on the safe side.

N: I'm fifty-seven years old . . .

V: Yes, I know, but I know that . . . You never know what you might . . . in our . . . in our situation. You can never be too sure. Probably in the glove compartment. I'll run out and get it. We don't have to use it. (SHORT PAUSE) I just have to say that you're as beautiful now as you were thirty years ago, when I saw you for the first time.

N: I am?

V: Yes, you are, truly and surely. (GIVES HER AN UNCERTAIN KISS. LEAVES.)

(N SITS STILL FOR A LITTLE WHILE, STANDS UP, PICKS UP HER THINGS, LOOKS AROUND AND LEAVES.)

DARKNESS.
LIGHT.

18.

E: Is that us?

F: Of course it is.

E: You and me?

F: Yes. You and me. (SILENCE) You didn't want to hold my hand. You didn't like that. You wanted to walk by yourself. I told you to hold my hand crossing the street, but you refused, you screamed and carried on. Finally I had to make you take my hand and you kept screaming and screaming. People looked at us. Finally I just gave up.

E: It sounds so sad.

F: Sugar sensitivity.

E: Sugar sensitivity?

F: Yes, you became a terror when you'd had too much sugar.

E: I don't think so.

F: Well, that's how it was.

E: It wasn't the sugar. (SILENCE) Where are we . . . over there?

F: There we were at his parents' house, Tobias' mother and father. I was with him at that time. Anyway, he was very kind. (SILENCE)

E: That's me.

F: Yes, that's you.

E: It's strange. (SILENCE)

F: I was younger then. I wanted to look like Harriet Andersson in *The Summer with Monika*. I bought a sweater just like hers. But he thought it was too tight on me. When we were going to see his parents.

E: Why don't we see . . .

F: See what?

E: How I am.

F: There are his two boys.

E: What has happened?

F: Charly and Niklas. Swimming. (SHORT PAUSE) They're swimming.

DARKNESS.
LIGHT.

19.

I: How are you feeling?

J: Well . . .

I: Good? Better?

J: I feel nauseous, but it doesn't matter.

I: I guess it'll get better after a while.

J: I don't know. Why would it?

I: What?

J: I haven't seen her for several days.

I: Who?

J: The one upstairs, the one who drinks. Maybe she's dead.

I: Yes, it was a while ago.

J: What?

I: That I saw her as well.

J: That's what I'm saying.

I: One never really sees her.

J: Maybe she's dead. What's that?

I: Ad inserts.

J: For what?

I: Who knows? (SILENCE) Why don't we post a message by our mailbox that we don't want any kind of advertising. Even though we've lived here for three years. (SILENCE) Tomorrow is Saturday.

J: I know.

I: I'm off from work.

J: Well, enjoy your day off. (SHORT PAUSE) Maybe she's dead. (SHORT PAUSE) She seems dead. When you see her. She kind of sneaks quietly by you . . . as if she didn't exist. Hardly ever says hello.

I: One has to ask oneself about what kind of life . . . she's living. (SHORT PAUSE) She hardly ever says hello.

J: That's what I said.

I: I've stopped saying hello myself. Why should I say hello to someone who doesn't say hello back to me?

J: Yesterday she said hello.

I: Why don't we do something tomorrow?

J: No.

I: Why not?

J: I can't. Not tomorrow. Tomorrow I'm going to Sofia. When I wake up. When I wake up. . . . I hardly ever sleep.

I: Aha.

J: It's as if she has some company when I'm there, when I sit by her and talk to her . . . so that she won't feel forgotten . . . and all alone. (SILENCE)

I: Sofia?

J: Today I thought that soon I should buy a little coat for her, because it's getting cold . . . and then I remembered. I remembered. (SILENCE) By now she would've been two years old. She would've been old enough to wear a coat. I saw a very nice one, light blue with mother of pearl buttons. In other countries it's important that the children are well dressed.

At times, not always. That the kids learn that they are valuable. She's the only thing I have.

I: We're having another one. A new one. A different one.

J: She's everything I have. The only thing I have.

I: We're going to have a new child. One who's alive.

J: We are?

I: You know we are.

J: I don't want that.

I: You already have one inside you.

J: It was created by a violent act.

I: Violent?

J: It was like a rape.

I: What the hell are you talking about?

J: Nothing will come of it. What could come of something that was created by violence?

DARKNESS.
LIGHT.

20.

O: What's going on?

H: It's too bright.

O: You can't just cover up the windows. Our windows.

H: Just for as long as I'm here.

O: Without even asking . . . You've got to take them down right now.

H: They are too close.

O: Too close? Who's too close?

H: The others.

O: Who?

H: All the others.

O: You can't do things like this.

H: I've already done it. (SILENCE)

O: Erik . . . Do you hear me?

H: No.

O: Anna. Come here. Hurry up!

P: (IS ON HER WAY.) What's going on?

O: Come in and I'll show you.

P: I'm coming, I'm coming. . . . What's going on? (COMES IN.)

O: He's covered the windows with blankets.

H: I just want a little peace and quiet. Once and for all. For me too.

O: This can't go on like this. Erik, you've got to think about your mother.

P: How long is this going to go on?

O: This is our home.

H: Human beings have created systems that rule our lives independently, systems that have made us slaves and can't be changed. We are slaves to an economy from hell, one single, huge capitalistic dictatorship. The social tensions are growing and getting worse every day. People starve in economic prisons. People have been robbed of the tools to make decisions of their own, about how to live, and of all their dignity and pride. We live like scared and threatened animals. We have to start riots to kill the Jacobeans, otherwise we'll silently go to pot, and everything that's worth saving will be destroyed. It'll be like the biggest concentration camp that ever was, whole countries will become concentration camps where nothing human is left and where there's no God. How could a God exist there?

P: Yes, dear, little Erik . . . everything will be all right.

H: We went to a therapist, the whore and I, to get some help with our so-called problems in our relationship, as if there would be a solution for them, the way this world looks, as if it would be possible to remain sane in this world. Suddenly I stood there holding a suitcase in my own home, as if it was a train station or an airport, without anywhere to go—and waiting for someone to explain things to me. Then I went to the ER in the psychiatric hospital and asked if I could talk to someone, because I knew I needed help. I don't know how long I was waiting. I talked to a woman who had a notebook where she wrote down everything going on, and she asked me if it's possible to be in two places at the same time. She read a few pages to me, where it said that she, on the same day at the same time, had been fucking a night watchman in a parking garage and also been in a bodega in Rhodes with her big brother. I can't really say that she was wrong.

O: You were just going to stay a few days.

P: What should we do?

O: I don't know. He has torn out our phone line.

H: I just want to be left alone and die like a human being.

P: You aren't going to die. What a silly thing to say.

O: You need help. (SILENCE) Erik . . . what did you do with the key to the door?

DARKNESS.
LIGHT.

21.

Q: This is good, right . . . in the shade. (SILENCE) Let's sit here for a while. . . . What do you think? (SILENCE) I think we should sit here for a while. I need a little rest. Sit down for a while. We don't have to go any further. (PAUSE) Nice day. Warm really. (SILENCE) Is everything OK with you? (Y LOOKS AT HIM) Well, I mean . . . is the sun in your eyes? (SILENCE) Isn't it good to be outside for a while in this nice weather? (SILENCE) To spend a little time in the park. It's bigger than you think. (SILENCE) Yes . . . Wait, I'll . . . (Y TURNS HIS HEAD AWAY.) I just want to . . . I want to wipe your face. (PAUSE) Just clean it. Nothing else. I used to do that when you were a little boy and had a dirty face. That's all. (SILENCE) (Y AND Q LOOK AT EACH OTHER.) (SILENCE) Yes. I know. (SILENCE) What can I say? What do you want me to say? (SHORT PAUSE) Yes, my God . . . (SILENCE) I can only . . . I didn't mean to . . . you understand, don't you?

Y: (MAKES LOUD SOUNDS.)

Q: I can only say . . . I tell myself that lower than that one can't go. Worse than what I've done. No one can tell me anything worse than what I've told myself. You have to know that! (SILENCE) But I can't . . . I can't leave you. I have to see you. You're the only one I have. The only one I have left. (SILENCE) You understand, don't you? (SILENCE) I've been alone every day since Elin died. (IT IS BEGINNING TO SNOW, SLOWLY AT FIRST, THEN HEAVIER AND HEAVIER.) It's been almost twenty years . . . this spring . . . (SILENCE) And I'm still young. Feeling young, anyway. (SILENCE) I don't ask you to ever forgive me . . . not now, not ever, but I still want you to try to understand how . . . weak I was, even though I fought against it . . . but it was much stronger than I am. It was as if I got my life back . . . as if my heart started to beat again . . . and then I don't know what happened . . . (SILENCE) Well, I'm being punished. (SHORT PAUSE) God knows what'll happen. (SILENCE) What's there to say? (SHORT PAUSE) What do you want me to say? I don't know. I don't know. (SILENCE) Well, I think . . . I think we should get going. We can't sit here any longer. I'll drive you home. Then I'll . . . when she gets back . . . I don't know if I . . . (STANDS UP AND BRUSHES SNOW FROM Y'S

SHOULDERS AND HANDS.) Oh yes, the ball . . . (BENDS DOWN AND PICKS UP THE BALL THAT Y IS USING TO WORK ON HIS MUSCLE STRENGTH.) I guess you need this one.

DARKNESS.
LIGHT.

ACT 3.

DARKNESS.
LIGHT.

1.

I: Why can't we go home?

J: Not yet.

I: There's nothing more to see.

J: Why don't you go home?

I: No. We just got here. (SILENCE)

V: It's getting a little cold.

L: Yes, now that there's no more fire.

F: It has probably burnt out.

L: Let's hope so.

F: It almost looked like a big bonfire at its peak. Only the singing was missing.

I: How long are we going to stay?

V: I guess this is it. I think they got to all the hot spots.

Q: Otherwise they wouldn't have dared to go inside.

D: There isn't much left.

Q: No, that's for sure.

I: (QUIETLY) I don't understand why you want to stand here and look at this. You didn't even want to go to the bonfire?

D: I wonder what started it?

V: We'll probably never know . . . with mysterious fires like these.

L: Hope that they had paid their insurance. (SILENCE)

D: What are they doing now?

V: Probably looking for something. That's what it looks like.

F: The ambulance is still here.

L: Let's just hope no one was home.

D: Yes, really.

F: You don't see them around very often.

L: No, that . . . that's for sure.

I: Can we go home now?

F: Not in the grocery store either.

L: That's a terrible store.

V: It's not a good store.

F: But still . . .

V: We don't shop there anymore.

L: I guess they appreciate a different kind of inventory.

F: Yes, you wonder what that might be. Strange that we hardly ever see them.

L: They keep to themselves.

V: A different culture.

L: Yes, maybe that's good. Just as well.

V: Different customs and habits. (SILENCE)

D: Hope they're away on vacation somewhere.

Q: It won't be much fun to come back to this.

L: No. They travel a lot. Are gone a lot.

F: I haven't seen them for quite a while. I don't remember when it was.

J: Maybe they're here.

I: Where?

V: Where?

J: The car is still here. It's in the garage.

Q: Yes, I see the car. A BMW.

V: Yes, where did the money come from?

L: Is the car without damage? (SILENCE)

D: What's happening?

V: What are they doing now? (SILENCE)

D: No . . .

F: Oh my God . . .

L: Yes . . . (SILENCE)

I: Let's go.

J: Leave me alone. (SILENCE)

L: Who is it? (SILENCE)

V: Can't really make it out.

DARKNESS.
LIGHT.

2.

A: It's me.

B: Yes, I know.

A: How's everything? Good?

B: Yes.

A: Good.

B: What do you want?

A: I just wanted to . . .

B: What?

A: I just wanted us to see each other.

B: You and me?

A: Yes.

B: So, here we are.

A: Yes. (SHORT PAUSE) Are you alone?

B: No, you're here.

A: Yes, but . . . Is he gone? Not at home?

B: No, he's in the bathroom.

A: He is? Aha.

B: You wouldn't be here if he was home, silly.

A: No, that's . . . that's what I thought.

B: That's what you thought?

A: Yes. (SILENCE)

B: Well?

A: (SHORT PAUSE) Well. I . . . I've been thinking of you.

B: You've been thinking of me?

A: Yes. Now and then.

B: Really. Thinking of me?

A: Yes. I want us to be together again, the two of us . . . like before. Like it was before. When we were together.

B: Before?

A: Yes, when we were together. Like it was then. You know what I mean.

B: Do you mean before you hit me?

A: Yes. No.

B: You know you hit me, right?

A: I didn't mean to. You know I didn't.

B: I know that you hit me, right in my face.

A: Yes, but I didn't mean to.

B: That was the end of that.

A: Yes. (SHORT PAUSE) Sure.

B: The end for me anyway . . . if you don't get it.

A: I know. But we . . . but before . . .

B: Once, and then never again.

A: Yes, I know. It'll never happen again.

B: You can be fucking sure of that.

A: That's what I'm saying. I know it's wrong . . . was wrong. I'm sorry.

B: Yes, maybe now you're getting it. What you didn't get before.

A: That's what I'm saying. I said I'm sorry. (SILENCE) But we belong together. You and me.

B: We do?

A: Now that I have a real job and everything. I've been taking classes. And also, we have a child.

B: A child?

A: Yes, we have a child. A kid.

B: A dead child. She died.

A: But we still have it. We had it.

B: It doesn't exist. It died before it was alive.

A: Anyway, we had it. For a little while. (SILENCE) I went there, where she is. On New Years Eve. Very peaceful.

B: Well, mine wasn't. (SILENCE)

A: So, what did you do on New Year's Eve?

B: Partied . . .

A: With him?

B: With everyone.

A: Sure. . . . Do you think about her?

B: No thanks. (B IS HOLDING SOMETHING THAT A SUDDENLY NOTICES.)

A: What is that?

B: It belongs to Arvid.

A: What Arvid?

B: Nick's kid. He's a boy. He's in a special class. He knows everything about birds and bird eggs and animals in the Azores, and he's helping out at the zoo.

DARKNESS.
LIGHT.

3.

J: It was very beautiful.

I: Beautiful?

J: Yes.

I: What was so beautiful?

J: Well, everything. They were.

I: You thought it was beautiful . . . a burnt down house?

J: Yes, when they carried them out. It was as if . . .

I: Beautiful?

J: Yes . . .

I: They were dead. Burned up.

J: Yes, but . . .

I: All three.

J: It was as if . . .

I: Three dead. Two were children . . . children that we know . . . seven years old, only seven years old, the little one, he was just seven years old.

J: Like in the Bible.

I: The Bible? (SHORT PAUSE) What fucking Bible?

J: Well, something that means something.

I: Like what? What does it mean? There were three people who died in the fire and we knew them, and they lived across the street—what does that mean?

J: Something big.

I: They are dead. . . . Ashes. Nothing more.

J: This was the first time something really happened. It was so real.

I: Yes indeed. (SILENCE)

J: We didn't really know them. One didn't get to know them.

I: We knew them enough.

J: I don't think I've said more than ten words to them during all these years since they moved in. (SILENCE) What did I say to them? Hello, have a nice day, the traffic is bad today. I guess that's basically all I've said to them. I don't even know what they did for a living.

I: What does it matter? (SILENCE)

J: I'll never forget what happened.

I: No, it . . .

J: The way I felt.

I: Felt?

J: The people's faces . . . how they looked, the ones who were watching.

I: You were there too.

J: Yes, how we looked. It was like a revelation. Like a day of reckoning. (SILENCE)

I: Even the old woman was there. (SILENCE) I don't understand how she has the money to still live here. We won't be able to stay here much longer. If something doesn't change. (PAUSE) We might have to move.

J: What does it matter?

DARKNESS.
LIGHT.

4.

D: Did you go?

C: This morning?

D: Yes. (SHORT PAUSE) How was it?

C: I don't know.

D: You don't know?

C: No.

D: I see.

C: (SILENCE) I can't . . .

D: No.

C: Do you understand?

D: Yes. Don't you think I do?

C: Yes . . . sure.

D: It's not hard to understand.

Ee: Daddy.

C: Yes.

Ee: I'm home.

C: Yes, I know.

Ee: Tomorrow we're going on a school trip.

C: Come here.

Ee: We're going to . . .

D: That night when Emma died . . . when she . . .

C: Wait, don't say anything.

D: Was that the night you were with me, and you called her? After the party, after the election? (SHORT PAUSE) I've got to know. Was it the same night?

C: I don't know.

D: Was it?

DARKNESS.
LIGHT.

5.

X: There. (SHORT PAUSE) Home. (SILENCE)

Y: It smells like smoke.

X: How are things? (SHORT PAUSE) Tired?

Y: Did you start to smoke? Have you been with someone who smokes?

X: That went OK.

Y: Answer me. (SILENCE) What's going on with you? (SHORT PAUSE) Tell me.

X: (STANDS UP, GOES UP TO HIM, STRAIGHTENS HIM OUT IN HIS CHAIR.) Don't you want to sit the way you're supposed to? (SHORT PAUSE) You were hanging. You could fall down. Down on the floor. (SHORT PAUSE) I don't think I could get you back in your chair.

Y: Take it easy.

X: (SILENCE) I haven't even taken off my coat. (SILENCE) How does it feel?

Y: Well, what the fuck do you think? (SHORT PAUSE) Like a guy sitting in a wheel chair.

X: Come on.

Y: How it feels? (SHORT PAUSE) It feels like I was in hell buried alive. As if I was buried alive. I feel like a fucking corpse.

X: To be home again?

Y: Buried alive. Buried inside myself. How the fuck do you think that feels?

X: Is it strange?

Y: I can't do anything myself. I can't even lift my hand. I can't piss or shit without getting help. I can't do anything.

X: To be home.

Y: Don't you understand?

X: It was a while ago. Almost a whole year.

Y: How the hell could you ask something that stupid?

X: It feels strange for me too.

Y: For you?

X: Yes, it feels strange. (SILENCE) I have to talk. I have to say something. Even though you can't answer me. I have to believe that you're answering me . . . somehow.

Y: Read my lips.

X: What?

Y: Read my lips.

X: (NOTICES SOMETHING THAT SHOULDN'T BE THERE.) Your dad brought it. He visited me the other day. He's so . . . (SILENCE) He just wanted to know if he could help with something, but I said that . . . I don't know what we'll need yet. (SHORT PAUSE) He had bought food . . . a turkey. (SILENCE) He wanted to be here tonight to welcome you back home, but I said that since it's your first night at home . . . (SILENCE) I'm thinking of giving the living room a new coat of paint, the walls and the ceiling. I've already bought the paint. (SHORT PAUSE) White.

DARKNESS.
LIGHT.

6.

F: Here it is.

Ee: I knew it was here.

F: Yes. (SILENCE)

Ee: I've been here five times.

F: With Daddy?

Ee: Yes. And with you. Once.

F: Yes, that's right. Put the flower just under the name. (Ee PUTS A WHITE FLOWER ON THE GRAVE STONE.) (SILENCE)

Ee: There are so many here.

F: Yes.

Ee: And all of them are dead.

F: Yes, they're all dead.

Ee: Like streets in a city . . . only names of dead people. (SILENCE) But Mommy hasn't been dead very long.

F: No, she . . .

EE: Are there any famous people here?

F: I don't know. I don't know who the famous people are.

Ee: Maybe they aren't famous any more. (SILENCE) (F TAKES Ee's HAND.) (SHORT PAUSE) Are you going to be here too when you're dead?

F: Well . . . I don't know. The sun is very strong.

Ee: Daddy wanted Mommy to be here, because it's close for us . . . to go and visit her. (SILENCE) Is there a soccer team with only seven fans?

F: Seven?

Ee: Yes.

F: Well . . . who knows? (SILENCE) Is she nice?

Ee: Veronika?

F: Yes.

Ee: I don't know . . . I don't care if she's nice. (SILENCE) I'm not going to call her Mommy. She said that herself. But he says "Daddy" to my daddy. But he's only five.

F: (SITS DOWN ON THE BENCH NEXT TO THE GRAVE.) You know, we should have brought something to eat. (SHORT PAUSE) Then we could have stayed a little longer. It's nice here in the sunshine.

DARKNESS.
LIGHT.

7.

N: This isn't the same room?

V: No, it isn't. (SHORT PAUSE) I hope you'll stay this time.

N: Yes, this time I will.

V: You're not running away this time?

N: No, I'm staying.

V: (SITS DOWN NEXT TO HER.) How are you?

N: Fine, thank you.

V: Feeling good? Had enough to eat?

N: Yes, thank you.

V: Well . . . (TAKES HER FOOT AND STARTS TO MASSAGE IT.)

N: Oh my God, that feels so good . . .

V: Your feet are so cute.

N: It feels wonderful . . . Heavenly . . .

V: Yes, it . . .

N: Yes . . . What are you thinking about? (SILENCE)

V: I'm thinking that . . . that it's been so long since I touched another human being. . . . I mean, in this way. . . . It just occurred to me now . . . how long it's been . . . in this way . . . and how long it's been since someone touched me . . . except doctors, of course . . . (SHORT PAUSE)

N: I know. (SILENCE)

V: What? Is it the fan?

N: (IS LOOKING FOR HER CELL PHONE.) Sorry. I just wanted to see if Emma had called. (SHORT PAUSE) No, she hasn't. (SHORT PAUSE) I don't dare to turn it off. I'm so worried about her.

V: Yes, I know . . . even though they are grown up and should be able to take care of themselves.

N: This morning she told me that Anders, her husband, has met another woman and wants a divorce. He just picked up and left her.

V: Do they have children?

N: Yes, a girl. Sanna. She's eight years old.

V: Yes, I know, I know how it is.

N: They've been together for ten years . . . they have a wonderful house with a garden and everything. I know how much work he's done in that house.

V: Well, it's . . .

N: And here we are.

V: Yes. But we aren't really hurting anyone.

N: Aren't we?

V: Are we? We, who have waited for so long. Almost a whole lifetime. (SILENCE)

N: What happened to your eye?

V: It's nothing. I had a little blood clot in my brain last fall, and they say that it isn't unusual to have a little bleeding now and then.

N: Does it hurt?

V: No, but it looks terrible. I have an appointment at the hospital next Tuesday. As long as it doesn't get any worse . . . nothing to worry about.

N: No. Wait. I'm just going to call and see if everything is OK.

V: Yes, just as well . . .

N: Yes. (PAUSE) Hello . . . Emma? (SHORT PAUSE) It's Mom. (PAUSE) What are you doing? (SHORT PAUSE) Were you asleep? (SHORT PAUSE) I can't hear what you're saying. . . . Hello. (SHORT PAUSE) Are you there? (SHORT PAUSE) Are you asleep? Emma? Answer me.

DARKNESS.
LIGHT.

8.

L: She's sleeping.

K: Thank God for that. (SILENCE)

L: You bought a new bed.

K: Yes, she needs a bigger one now. She's too big for the other one.

L: How quickly they grow . . . When will you be back?

K: I told you.

L: When, did you say?

K: Around eleven. (SILENCE)

L: Why are you so dressed up?

K: I am?

L: The earrings.

K: Yes, I know.

L: I gave them to you on your thirtieth birthday.

K: Yes, that was then.

L: Do you have to wear them tonight?

K: Why shouldn't I?

L: Since you're meeting someone. On a date.

K: It's just someone from work. He wants to know what I think of . . .

L: His cock. His big cock.

K: I can hear that you have a real problem.

L: I do?

K: You don't have to stand there and look at me.

L: No, you're right. I don't have to. (SILENCE)

K: I'll call you if I'll be late.

L: You said eleven.

K: If I happen to be a few minutes late. Eleven is like the middle of the night when you haven't been out of the house for three years.

L: Sure.

K: I need a couple of hours to just breathe and meet other grownups.

L: Yes, of course you do.

K: I'm with her from morning to night.

L: I know.

K: No, you don't know. Every fucking day and night for three years.

L: Yes.

K: Am I right?

DARKNESS.
LIGHT.

9.

(A GROUP OF PEOPLE WEARING UGLY, STRANGE NEON-COLORED CLOTHES ARE SITTING IN A DILAPIDATED ROOM IN A SEMICIRCLE IN FRONT OF AN OLD TV SET, WHERE A PROGRAM WITH ACROBATIC DANCING IS GOING ON. YOUNG, MUSCLED PEOPLE ARE SWIRLING AROUND WEARING TIGHT, PROVOCATIVE COSTUMES.)

G: Today is the longest day of the year.

S: To hell with it.

G: It just came to me.

S: To me, too . . . Didn't you hear me? I don't see very well anymore.

G: No, you don't. You only see when you want to see.

S: Why are you pointing your finger?

G: I'm not pointing. It's pointing.

S: You're pointing it straight into my eye. My eye. If I lean forward.

G: I've got a straight finger. What the hell, it's a work injury.

S: Not my problem. Why don't you turn the other way?

G: Then I can't see.

S: Not much to see anyway.

G: It's God's finger. It's pointing out the way.

S: The way?

G: Yes, the way.

S: It's just a corridor.

G: The longest day of the year.

S: What about it?

G: It's longer . . . than the other days.

S: Yes.

H: Well, it's not easy to live together. Everybody knows that.

S: No, it's easier to die. You need some kind of structure, a framework.

G: Did we eat? Did we eat today?

S: Yes, I think so.

G: What did we have?

S: Some kind of fish. Now your finger is in my eye again.

H: When a world is as ugly as this one, I'd rather look the other way.

G: You don't know what you're talking about. You don't exist.

H: Yes I do. I'm a human being, a thinking, living creature, compared to you, an educated and respected individual among the people who count, and a member of society who has lived a successful and, in every way, prosperous life.

G: You, an individual?

H: If you by any chance might know what that is.

G: And what do you think I am then?

H: I don't think I have enough imagination to try to characterize what you are. I'm not supposed to be here. I'm really not supposed to be here!

G: Where are you supposed to be then?

DARKNESS.
LIGHT.

10.

(Y IS SITTING IN HIS WHEEL CHAIR, LISTENING TO HIS IPHONE, WEARING EARBUDS. SHE SPEAKS TO THE AUDIENCE.) (BLACK SNOW)

B: (IS WITH THE PARALYZED CELLIST IN THE PARK.) (SILENCE) (LIGHTS A CIGARETTE.) My brother is also paralyzed. He's my oldest brother. I haven't told you that. He's in a wheel chair too, but he can talk. If there's someone to talk to. I don't know. I don't think so. It's been a while since I saw him. Five years. I guess there's someone who takes care of him now and then, like what I'm doing with you.

Someone giving him wood and stuff. But I don't know how he's doing, I don't even know if he's alive. But I would've heard I guess. He's much older than me. I don't see my dad either. Now he's very old, retired. Still lives where he used to live. Why am I thinking about him? I usually don't think about him. Your dad seems like a nice guy. At least he visits you now and then. He never gets in touch with me, so why should I? Since he's not interested in me. He wasn't interested in us when we were little either. (Y IS MOVING WITH THE MUSIC.) Mom made us a family. When she died everything like crashed. I was eleven then, when she died. My oldest brother had his own apartment then. Not where he's living now. The funeral was beautiful. I sang. I sang a song she loved, "Mountain High." And my brother was allowed to sit in the front seat of the hearse.

11.

R: Is that the radio? (SHORT PAUSE) Is it on? That's talking?

GIRL'S VOICE: It's me.

R: Is that you?

GIRL'S VOICE: Yes . . . what are you doing?

R: I've told you . . . I don't want anyone here. I want to be left alone. I have the right to be alone.

GIRL'S VOICE: Really. But it's just us.

R: Us?

GIRL'S VOICE: You and me.

R: Go someplace else. Go to your own mom.

GIRL'S VOICE: She's working . . . my mom is working.

R: Yes, she's working. One has to work.

GIRL'S VOICE: So that we have food and clothes. Otherwise we'd be starving.

R: I've worked every day of my life, every fucking day. Then I got married. . . . I cooked and cleaned and took care of everything . . . twice . . . with two different men. (SILENCE) Now I just want to be left alone.

GIRL'S VOICE: You're not allowed to drink anymore.

R: Yes, I am. As much as I want.

GIRL'S VOICE: No.

R: Yes I am. It's my life.

GIRL'S VOICE: No.

R: I can do whatever I want. I've paid for every drop with my own money.

GIRL'S VOICE: You'll die.

R: Yes, that's what I want. I want to die.

GIRL'S VOICE: Then I'll die too, if you die.

R: You? You're just a little girl.

GIRL'S VOICE: I'll die too. I don't want to die.

R: No, only me. . . . Only me. Only me. Then I don't have to deal with this. (SILENCE) Why aren't you outside playing . . . with the others?

GIRL'S VOICE: I've no one to play with.

R: Me neither. (SILENCE)

GIRL'S VOICE: You look ugly when you drink. You smell bad. You smell like poop.

DARKNESS.
LIGHT.

12.

K: Hello. . . . (SILENCE) Where are you? Are you here?

L: Yes. (PAUSE) I fell asleep. (SILENCE)

K: Is she sleeping?

L: I think so. What time is it?

OO: Hi, there.

K: This is Patrik.

OO: Robert. Hi.

K: We work together.

OO: In the same place.

K: Was she sleeping all night?

L: Yes.

K: Good. Good for you, I mean. (SILENCE) What have you been doing?

L: Well . . .

K: Did you watch TV?

L: No, it . . .

OO: I don't think we've met before?

K: No, you haven't. This is the first time.

OO: I'm sure I would remember.

L: I hope so.

K: Come in.

OO: Well I . . . What a great chair.

K: Yes, I bought it in a little store that was about to go out of business.

OO: Really very nice.

K: Yes, I like it.

OO: Looks like industrial design.

K: Yes. And here it looks like . . . . like a single mom living with her three-year-old.

OO: Yes, I know . . . I know how it is.

K: Her building blocks and her stuffed animals take up all the room, like a real tsunami.

OO: Yes, that's how it is . . . (PAUSE)

K: It was great that you could baby sit for a couple of hours.

L: What do you mean by that?

K: Aren't you going home now?

L: Are you drunk?

K: Sorry?

L: Well?

K: Drunk?

L: Yes.

K: What do you mean by that? I had a glass of wine. I drank a glass of wine.

L: One?

K: Yes, one glass in three hours.

OO: Yes, I can vouch for that.

L: Why don't you shut up.

K: Why don't you fucking leave.

DARKNESS.
LIGHT.

13.

(N IS SITTING QUIETLY IN A BIG, WHITE ROOM. V GOES UP TO HER, DOESN'T KNOW WHAT TO SAY. N SLOWLY LOOKS UP AT HIM, STARTS TO SMILE, THEN STOPS SMILING.)

V: I just wanted to say that it was . . . Well, I wanted to be here anyway, but I didn't want to . . . so I stayed in the back, all the way in the back.

N: I felt that you were here.

V: I sat in the back. (SILENCE) (TAKES HER HAND.) It was very beautiful.

N: She was a beautiful human being.

V: Yes, I'm sure. I'm sure she was. (SILENCE) Is there anything I can do?

N: No. Absolutely not. Nothing at all.

V: No, I . . .

N: I have nothing left. She was the only thing that was important to me. Why I stayed. Why I didn't leave when I should have left. What good did it do?

V: No, that . . . one never knows. (SILENCE)

N: I am going to leave him.

V: You are?

N: Yes. Let's go.

V: Now? Here?

N: Yes. Let's go now. He can take whatever he wants. I'll pick up the rest tomorrow. I have to be with someone who's alive. Let's go. I'll bring the Bible. I even stole a Bible from the room in the motel that night when we . . . well . . . I don't know what's wrong with me.

DARKNESS.
LIGHT.

14.

(SEVEN PEOPLE ARE SITTING IN EITHER A SUBWAY CAR OR IN THE CAR OF A TRAIN THAT HAS BEEN BURNED IN A FIRE. PARTS OF THEIR BODIES AND THEIR CLOTHING ARE BURNED AS WELL. THEY ARE PARTLY COVERED BY ASHES AND THERE IS A STILLNESS SURROUNDING THEM. EVERYTHING AROUND THEM HAS BEEN BURNED, HAS MELTED, BEEN BLASTED AWAY INTO PIECES.)

O: I don't see anything.

C: Is there anything wrong with your eyes?

O: Yes, they can't see.

H: Does it hurt?

S: Yes.

H: Still?

S: Yes.

H: I thought it would pass after a while. I thought we would keep our arms and legs anyway.

S: Yes, I think these are mine.

G: Normally it only takes me forty minutes during rush hour to get home, from the time I leave my office to the time I open the door where I live. I would've been home by now. Would have made myself a sandwich and poured myself a glass of beer, and checked if there was any mail, but there never is, nowadays, and my wife would have had time to put on her coat and run to a meeting at the office of the city council. She is a member of the social service committee.

A: I don't often think of the child that died, the one we had, but died a couple of hours later. I don't think about it a lot these days, since it was many years ago, but in the beginning I was wondering what would have happened if it had made it, if Nike and I would still be together. But one will never know. There's a lot one will never know, but that doesn't mean one can't wonder about it. (PAUSE)

S: Your pants are torn.

A: It's supposed to be that way.

J: I have to pick up my daughter.

S: Yes.

J: She's in daycare.

S: She is? I see.

J: In preschool. They close at five o'clock and I told them this morning that I would pick her up already at two today, after their snack, since I stopped work earlier. I was going to be there as soon as they had had their snacks. But now I can't do that. It's almost six o'clock. And she's there alone. There's no one else who can pick her up. Who would that be? They close already at five. She thinks that I'm going to be there. She usually says "Mommy is coming, mommy is working, but mommy is coming, mommy is coming soon. Mommy will be here." She gets so happy when I get there to pick her up.

C: The whole time I hear what Emma once said, when she was in the hospital: "I've never been happy. Not one day in my whole life. I've just been pretending," she said.

V: There's always someone missing. Someone who isn't there. Who should be there. Whether I'm thinking of her or not thinking of her, it's her I'm thinking about. It's the same thing. She's more present . . . because she isn't present . . .

F: Now they are playing music!

G: I don't hear anything.

F: You don't hear the music?

G: No.

DARKNESS.
LIGHT.

15.

B: Is that you?

A: Yes.

B: Really . . .

A: Well, I thought I'd come by. (SILENCE) Is it over?

B: I hope so.

A: Aha . . . what is it?

B: A kid.

A: Girl?

B: No, a boy.

A: Aha. (SILENCE)

B: Are those for me?

A: Yes, I bought them downstairs, where you enter. You've got to bring something.

B: Thank you.

A: I think I'll sit here. (SITS DOWN ON THE BED.) So, is everything OK?

B: No, how could it be? (SILENCE)

A: What's . . .

B: How the fuck would I know.

A: No. . . . Wasn't he with you?

B: No.

A: Really. I was with you. (SHORT PAUSE) When are you going home?

B: Tomorrow.

A: So soon?

B: Yes, but where will I go?

A: Where?

B: I have nowhere to go.

A: You have nowhere to go?

B: No, it was his apartment. I can't go there. I don't want to either.

A: No.

B: I'd rather die.

A: What are you going to do?

B: I don't know. (SILENCE) I guess social services will help in the beginning. I'm talking to some fucking welfare worker this afternoon. She was in here this morning, sighing.

A: I see.

B: But I was too tired to talk to her. (SILENCE) You always know what they want to do.

A: Yes, it's . . .

B: It'll probably be some rotten studio apartment somewhere. (SILENCE)

A: You could live with me.

B: With you?

A: Yes, I have room.

B: For what? (SILENCE)

A: I have two rooms.

B: Yes, I know.

A: You could live there until . . . well, however long . . . as long as you want to . . . if you want to. (SILENCE) As long as you want to.

B: I can?

A: I've got plenty of space. I could take off a couple of days if you need anything.

B: What would I need?

A: Well, I don't know . . . for the kid.

B: No.

A: Maybe a stroller . . . Do you have one?

B: I have nothing. I only have the clothes I'm wearing.

A: You'll need a crib. (SILENCE) I've got a job and everything.

DARKNESS.
LIGHT.

16.

(A VERY BIG GROCERY STORE)

Q: (SILENCE) Is that you?

X: Yes, I need to find the pasta. It's usually here somewhere.

Q: I'm looking for it too.

X: I'm looking for the fresh kind . . . but I can't find it. It's probably in some other place. I guess they've changed everything around again.

Q: Yes, fresh tastes much better.

X: How are things?

Q: Everything's fine . . . it's nice to see you.

X: They change things around all the time.

Q: I'm shopping for food for John. I think we'll have spaghetti and meat sauce tonight.

X: Yes, that's easy enough.

Q: Easier for him to eat. (SILENCE)

X: I don't know what we'll have tonight.

Q: No, sometimes it's hard to come up with anything new. (SILENCE)

X: How's he doing?

Q: How's he doing? No real change, really. I can't say there's been much of a change. We just try to go forward.

X: Yes.

Q: Anyway, it doesn't seem to get any worse. He can say a few more words now, but no one understands him. I heard you had a baby.

X: Yes.

Q: Do you live around here?

X: Yes, behind the church.

Q: Oh, up there. That's very nice.

X: My husband is a minister in that church.

Q: He is? A minister?

X: Yes. (SILENCE) It was good to see you.

Q: Yes.

X: Please say hello to John. (SILENCE)

Q: Yes, John . . . I think he misses you.

X: Tell him hello from me.

Q: Why don't we go out there and have a cup of coffee?

X: No, that's not possible.

Q: No, it . . . (SILENCE) He hates me. But I'm the only one he has.

DARKNESS.
LIGHT.

17.

I: Are you here? (SHORT PAUSE) Hello, hey you. (SILENCE) Joanna. (SILENCE) Joanna? (SHORT PAUSE) I'm here. (SILENCE)

J: Yes.

I: Well, I . . . Why don't you say hello? Just hello.

J: Hello.

I: How are you? (IS ABOUT TO TAKE HER HAND, BUT SHE DOESN'T WANT HIM TO, THEN ALLOWS HIM TO HOLD IT AS IF IT DIDN'T BELONG TO HER.) I just want to hold your hand.

J: Be my guest.

I: (SHORT PAUSE) How's today going?

J: What do you want?

I: What I want?

J: What do you want?

I: What do you mean? (SHORT PAUSE) Nothing. I want to see you.

J: Aha.

I: Talk to you. Be here with you.

J: Yes, there's so much talking. If you're quiet, you still hear them talking.

I: Who?

J: What day is it today?

I: What day is it? It's Sunday . . . Sunday the fourteenth.

J: (PICKS UP HER NOTE BOOK AND STARTS WRITING.)

I: We miss you. Josefin and I. We miss you. She wanted to come and see you, but I don't know if that's good for her. What are you writing?

J: I write down what I have to remember.

I: What? What do you need to remember?

J: Important things.

I: Well, that's good.

J: So I won't forget.

I: Yes. (SILENCE) She'll be three years old on Saturday. (SILENCE) Yesterday we went to the Zoo. I didn't think it would be that crowded, but it was terrible. Mostly tourists. Could hardly move. I felt like I was going to have a panic attack, but I'm sure she had fun. (SILENCE) They must make a bundle. Ninety bucks just to get in.

J: It might be cheaper with a yearly card.

I: Yes. Do you think you will be able to come home for a while on Saturday, for her birthday? Just for a couple of hours?

J: No.

I: For a couple of hours? I'll pick you up and drive you back.

J: No.

I: Couldn't you try, for her sake?

J: No.

I: She misses you. I miss you.

J: Why don't you call a cab?

DARKNESS.
LIGHT.

18.

P: Finally he's at rest.

T: Yes.

P: He just fell asleep they said.

T: Was there anyone with him?

P: I don't know . . . but I'll ask. Doesn't he look much younger? The way he looked before.

T: Yes, maybe so.

P: (TO X, WHO IS NOW LIVING WITH THE MINISTER.) You never had a chance to get to know him before he got so sick . . .

X: No, I didn't.

P: He wasn't the same person. It was as if something had destroyed everything I had fallen in love with. It was the way a fire destroys a whole house and only ashes remain . . . But he was still there, in some way. (SILENCE) It's as if he is here now.

T: He is.

X: Yes. His spirit is. (SILENCE)

T: We should gather up his possessions.

H: What did he have?

T: I don't know. Not very much.

H: Nothing.

P: His clothes. Nothing else I don't think.

T: He is our father.

H: No, he isn't.

P: Can't we just sit here silently for a little while . . .

X: I have to leave soon. I have to pick up Joshua from daycare.

P: Yes, why don't all of you go ahead? I want to sit here for a while alone with him.

H: Why do you want to do that?

T: Yes, we understand.

X: Is there anything we can do?

P: No, no. Everything is done. (SILENCE) I just want to sit here quietly.

H: Yes, OK. (WALKS UP TO THE DEAD MAN.) Well, I never knew you. And you didn't know me either. You were my father, but that was about it. Otherwise, or most of the time, you were a fucking, narrow-minded idiot filled with empty opinions about everything you didn't have a clue about. I can't say that I'm grieving, because you've been dead as long as I can remember, at least to me. We tried, I guess, but it didn't work. Finally I realized that there wasn't any chance that we would have a real connection. I'm not even feeling any relief. I don't feel anything, really.

P: Please leave.

H: Yes, I'm leaving. I'm on my way.

P: Please leave now.

H: Sure.

P: Thank you.

(SILENCE) (P IS SITTING STILL FOR A WHILE. ALONE. THEN SHE STANDS UP AND GOES AND LIES IN THE BED NEXT TO O. SHE EMBRACES HIM. SHE BREATHES ON HIM.)

DARKNESS.
LIGHT.

19.

L: This is terrible.

V: Yes, it really is . . .

I: How long is it going to remain like this . . .

V: Well, who knows?

I: You don't want to even look at it while driving by.

V: And yet you can't avoid it.

L: It destroys the whole neighborhood. It's probably going to bring down the value of the other houses by hundreds of thousands. Who wants to live next to a grave?

D: I guess they'll rebuild at some point.

L: Who? Who would that be?

D: Those who . . . the owners.

U: She's in a mental hospital and the others are dead.

F: She is? Where?

U: Magdalena told me. She and Peter had visited her last Saturday. They were friends . . . and that's understandable . . . when you have nothing left.

D: (SILENCE) How was she?

U: How she was? How can someone be, who's lost her husband and two sons?

D: No, that . . . (SILENCE)

U: She's going to write a book.

I: A book?

U: She's going to write about what happened. What she has experienced. About her experiences. Her doctor advised her to do it. About her childhood and the Balkan war, about how it was to flee from her homeland and all that. Write about everything, both before and after.

L: I guess that could be interesting for people who are interested. To know more. . . . But I think that we already know so much about everything . . . we're already informed.

DARKNESS.
LIGHT.

20.

(Y IS SITTING ALONE UP FRONT IN THE BIG, WHITE ROOM, PLAYING THE CELLO, A FEW MINUTES OF MUSIC BY BACH.)

DARKNESS.
LIGHT.

THE END

Major Plays by Lars Norén

1979	ORESTES
1981	A TERRIBLE HAPPINESS
1981	MUNICH – ATHENS
1981	SMILES OF THE INFERNO
1982	NIGHT IS MOTHER TO THE DAY
1982	CHAOS IS THE NEIGHBOR OF GOD
1982	DEMONS
1983	THE LAST SUPPER
1984	CLAUDIO (MANTEGNA PORTOFOLIO)
1985	THE COMEDIANS
1986	FLOWERS OF OUR TIME
1987	HEBRIANA
1988	AUTUMN AND WINTER
1988	BOBBY FISCHER LIVES IN PASADENA
1988	AND GIVE US THE SHADOWS
1989	TRUTH OR DARE
1989	SUMMER
1990	LOVE MADE SIMPLE
1990	CHINNON
1991	THE LAST QUARTET
1991	LOST AND FOUND
1991	THE LEAVES IN VALLOMBROSA
1992	MOIRE DI –
1992	STERBLICH
1994	ROMANIANS
1994	BLOOD
1994	A KIND OF HADES
1994	THE CLINIC
1994	TRIO TO THE END OF THE WORLD
1997	PERSONKRETS 3:1
1998	SEVEN/THREE
1998	SHADOW BOYS
2000	NOVEMBER
2000	ACT
2000	COMING AND GOING

2002   QUIET WATERS
2003   DETAILS
2003   CHILL
2005   WAR
2006   TERMINAL
2007   ANNA POLITKOVSKIA
2010   ORESTIEN
2012   FRAGMENTE
2013   3.31.93.

Acknowledgments

My heartfelt "thank you" to my husband, Len, for supporting and helping me every day of my life. Without him there would be no books—no life.

Many, many thanks to Richard and Jane Altschuler for their unending care, guidance and friendship.

My deep gratitude to Bo Corre for her constant support—especially for producing a wonderful reading of 3.31.93. in New York City in 2014; and many thanks to all of the participating great actors—and to Sofia Jupither, for flying in from Stockholm to direct the reading, and Ulrika Josephsson, for joining Sofia and bringing a giant poster of Lars Norén.

Finally, a warm "thank you" to Margareta Petersson in Stockholm, for all her help and assistance with just about everything Norén.

www.ingramcontent.com/pod-product-compliance
Lightning Source LLC
Chambersburg PA
CBHW021056080526
44587CB00010B/260